THE CALVARY ROAD

ROY HESSION

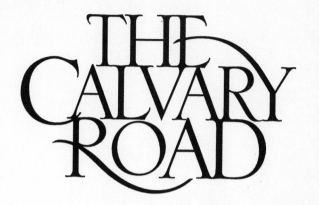

THE CALVARY ROAD

ROY HESSION

CLC ❖ PUBLICATIONS
Fort Washington, Pennsylvania 19034

Published by CLC ❖ Publications

U.S.A.
P.O. Box 1449, Fort Washington, PA 19034

GREAT BRITAIN
51 The Dean, Alresford, Hants. SO24 9BJ

AUSTRALIA
P.O. Box 419M, Manunda, QLD 4879

NEW ZEALAND
10 MacArthur Street, Feilding

ISBN 0-87508-236-X

·Contents·

· Introduction ·

I am sure from my own experience, as well as from what we have seen in the ranks of our Mission these last three years, that what the authors tell us about in these pages is one of God's vital words to His worldwide church today. For long I had regarded revival only from the angle of some longed-for, but very rare, sudden outpouring of the Spirit on a company of people. I felt that there was a missing link somewhere. Knowing of the continuing revival on a certain mission field, and because it was continuing and not merely sudden and passing, I long felt that they had a further secret we needed to learn. Then the chance came for heart-to-heart fellowship with them, first through one of our own missionary leaders whose life and ministry had been transformed by a visit to that field, and then through conferences with some of their missionaries on furlough, and finally through the privilege of having two of the national

brethren living for six months at our head-
quarters.

From them I learned and saw that revival
is first personal and immediate. It is the constant experience of any simplest Christian
who "walks in the light," but I saw that walking in the light means an altogether new sensitiveness to sin—a calling things by their
proper name of sin, such as pride, hardness,
doubt, fear, self-pity, which are often passed
over as merely human reaction. It means a
readiness to "break" and confess at the feet
of Him who was broken for us, for the blood
does not cleanse excuses, but always cleanses
sin, confessed as sin; then revival is just the
daily experience of a soul full of Jesus and
running over.

Further, we are beginning to learn, as a
company of Christ's witnesses, that the riv-
ers of life to the world do not flow out in their
fullness through one man, but through the
body, the team. Our brokenness and openness must be two-way, horizontal as well as
vertical, with one another as with God. We
are just beginning to experience in our own
ranks that teamwork in the Spirit is one of
the keys to revival, and that we have to learn
and practice the laws of a living fellowship.

I need not say more, as Roy Hession and

his wife expound the whole matter. But we have seen God at work in our midst. I could name half-a-dozen of our workers, several of them leaders, in whose lives there has been a new spiritual revolution. Then rivulets of blessing in some of our individual lives have been merging in a larger stream. God has been giving us times as a company when "as they prayed, the place was shaken where they were assembled together, and they were all filled with the Holy Ghost." Here and there on our battlefields, distant and near, the sound of abundance of rain is being heard; and we believe among many companies of God's people He is preparing afresh for these last days a "sharp threshing instrument having teeth," and that what God is saying to us through this revival, and through the interpretation of that message in this book, is a word of the Lord for our day. May it be greatly used to produce revived lives, revived fellowships, and revived churches.

NORMAN P. GRUBB
Honorary Secretary
Worldwide Evangelization Crusade
London, 1950

· Preface to the 1973 Edition ·

This little book was first published some twenty-three years ago. With the passage of years I am more sure now than even then that the truths expressed in these pages lie at the heart of all those movements of revival by which God has restored His church to new life in the hours of her dryness and need. Such movements of revival are not only glorious memories of the past, but are taking place right now in various parts of the world. The outward forms of such revivals do, of course, differ considerably, but the inward and permanent content of them all is always the same: a new experience of conviction of sin among the saints; a new vision of the cross of Jesus and of redemption; a new willingness on man's part for brokenness, repentance, confession, and restitution; a joyful experience of the power of the blood of Jesus to cleanse fully from sin and restore and heal all that that sin has lost and broken; a new entering into the fullness of the Holy Spirit and of His power to do His own work through His people; and a new gathering in of the lost ones to Jesus. Inasmuch as this is just what is happening now in various parts of the world, these pages have a special relevance for the reader today and I trust may by the blessing of God be the means of helping many another to come to the cross and present himself as a candidate for revival by the confession of his emptiness and failure. For revival is not a green valley getting greener, but a valley full of dry bones being made to live again and stand up an exceeding great army (Ezek. 37). It is not good Christians becoming better Christians—as God sees us there are not any good Christians—but rather Christians honestly confessing that their Christian life is a valley of dry bones and by that very confession qualifying for the grace that flows from the cross and makes all things new.

This little book expresses the truths that lie at the heart of revival just because it is itself the product of revival. As long ago as 1930 God began to work in a new way in the infant church in Rwanda, East Africa. Infant that it was it carried the seeds of decay within it, but a decay which God began to change into glorious fruitage when revival came. In the years that followed, the blessing of revival spread to the churches in the neighboring countries of Uganda, Kenya, and Tanzania. A great multitude of Africans, and missionaries among them, not only came to know Christ as their personal Saviour, but began to live a quality of life rarely experienced in even the most evangelical churches of the West. That movement of revival has continued in East Africa to the present day, if not in one part then in another, with all the vicissitudes and battles that one would naturally expect of a movement of life.

In 1947 I had been doing full-time evangelistic work in Great Britain for a number of years, but had come into a state of great spiritual need. I had somehow lost the power of the Holy Spirit which I once had known in the work of the Lord and yet I had to continue to conduct evangelistic campaigns without His power—a terrible experience! I was rather like that son of the prophets in Elisha's school who lost his axe-head while chopping down a tree, but who perhaps for a few strokes at least continued to chop with just the handle and wondered why he was making no progress with his work! Ignorant of what had really happened I redoubled my efforts and became increasingly tense and forceful, all of which was a poor substitute for the Spirit's gentle penetrating power. It is, of course, in looking back that I can describe my situation in this way. At the time I was all too ignorant of my need.

In April 1947 I invited several missionaries from East Africa to come as speakers to an Easter Conference which I was organizing, because I had heard that they had been experiencing revival in their field for a number of years, and as an evangelist I was interested in revival. What they had to say was very different from much of what I had associated with that word. It was very simple and very quiet. As they unfolded their message and gave their testimonies, I discovered that I was the neediest person in the conference, and was far more in need of being revived than I had ever realized. That discovery, however, came only slowly to me. Being myself one of the speakers, I suppose I was more concerned about others' needs than my own. As my wife and others humbled themselves before God and experienced the cleansing of the blood of Jesus, I found myself left somewhat high and dry—dry just because I was high. I was humbled by the simplicity of the message, or rather the simplicity of what I had to do to be revived and filled with the Spirit. When at the end of the conference others testified as to how Jesus had broken them at His cross and filled their hearts to overflowing with His Spirit, I had no such testimony. It was only afterwards that I was enabled to give up trying to fit things into my doctrinal scheme and come humbly to the cross for cleansing from my own personal sins. It was like beginning my Christian life all over again. My flesh "came again like that of a little child," as did Naaman's when he was willing to humble himself and dip himself in Jordan. It has been an altogether new chapter in life since then. It has meant, however, that I have had to choose constantly to die to the big "I" that Jesus might be all, and constantly to come to Him for cleansing in His precious blood. But that is why it is a new chapter.

The things learned at that time and in the months that followed were committed to paper and were published mostly as articles, later to be collected together to form this book. In the years that have followed its publication, its distribution has spread throughout the whole English-speaking world and it has been translated into some forty languages—to the astonishment of no one more than the one who penned it. Its wide dissemination is simply the evidence of the hunger of Christians throughout the world for reality and a Christianity that really works. More than that, it is one of many evidences that "the time to favour Zion, even the set time, has come" (Psalm 102:13), and that God's purpose to build again "the walls of Jerusalem that are broken down" (Neh. 2:13) is coming to pass.

It must not be thought that this book represents a purely personal contribution on my part. The things recorded in this book have been learned in fellowship with others in various parts who have begun to walk the Way of the Cross in a new way. Any one of a number in that fellowship might have written these chapters equally well. It is a fellowship, too, that is continually growing, for an ever-increasing number of lives have been greatly influenced right across the world, as teams have gone to this and that country and numerous tours have been undertaken. This fact, I think, adds to the strength and significance of what is here written. One realizes, of course, that this stream of blessing of which one has been a part is but one of a number of streams of new life, all of which emanate from the same source of the cross and are contributing to the deeply needed revival of the church.

Leaving the mountain, the streamlet grows,
 Flooding the vale with a river;
So, from the hill of the cross, there flows
 Life more abundant for ever.

Over the years some have occasionally queried the use of the term "revival" to describe the sort of message and experience expressed in this book, pointing to the fact that they cannot see any spectacular religious awakening, involving great numbers of people, with many turning to the Lord, such as is popularly associated with the word "revival." Somehow we have never been able to accede to this objection. Rather, we would doggedly insist that the things we have been learning over these years, some of which are written in these chapters, are the very essence of revival and would, if widely responded to and deeply applied, result indeed in the widest revival of the church—as wide as the response to the call to brokenness at the cross is wide. Certainly for those who have humbled themselves under the hand of God at that place where sins are washed away, it has meant the revival of their Christian lives in the truest and simplest sense of the word. There are indeed now ever-expanding beachheads of revival in many hearts, in many fellowships and many churches and in various lands. It is for those in whose hearts Jesus has established such beachheads to hold fast the vision that what they have discovered and are continually discovering in experience is revival indeed, and to know that God's establishment of such beachheads is surely but the prelude for His invasion in mighty and wide-ranging power into our situations of need. As I write, heartening news comes that His invasions in power are in fact occuring in this and that place and God is reviving His church in this wider way according to His sovereign grace. May we be willing in this the day of His power!

This leads me to say a word about the necessary attitude of heart for the reader. If God is to bless him at all through these pages he must come to them with a deep hunger of heart. He must be possessed with a dissatisfaction of the state of the church in general, and of himself in particular—especially of himself. He must be willing for God to begin His work in himself first, rather than in the other man. He must, moreover, be possessed with the holy expectancy that God can and will meet his need. If he is in any sense a Christian leader, the urgency of the matter is intensified many times over. His willingness to admit his need and be blessed will determine the degree to which God can bless the people to whom he ministers. Above all, he must realize that he must be the first to humble himself at the cross. If a new honesty with regard to sin is needed among his people, he must begin with himself. It was when the King of Nineveh arose from his throne, covered himself with sackcloth, and sat in ashes as a sign of his repentance, that his people repented.

Let not, however, those readers who are not leaders be tempted to look at those who are and wait for them. God wants to begin with each one of us. He wants to begin with *you*.

May God bless us all.

ROY HESSION
February 1973

· 1 ·

Brokenness

We want to be very simple in this matter of revival. Revival is just the life of the Lord Jesus poured into human hearts. Jesus is always victorious. In heaven they are praising Him all the time for His victory. Whatever may be our experience of failure and barrenness, He is never defeated. His power is boundless. And we, on our part, have only to get into a right relationship with Him and we shall see His power being demonstrated in our hearts and lives and service, and His victorious life will fill us and overflow through us to others. And that is revival in its essence.

If, however, we are to come into this right relationship with Him, the first thing we must learn is that our wills must be broken to His will. To be broken is the beginning of revival. It is painful, it is humiliating, but it is the only way. It is being "Not *I*, but Christ,"[1] and a

[1] Gal. 2:20.

"C" is a bent "I." The Lord Jesus cannot live in us fully and reveal Himself through us until the proud self within us is broken. This simply means that the hard unyielding self, which justifies itself, wants its own way, stands up for its rights, and seeks its own glory, at last bows its head to God's will, admits its wrong, gives up its own way to Jesus, surrenders its rights and discards its own glory—that the Lord Jesus might have all and be all. In other words, it is dying to self and self-attitudes.

And as we look honestly at our Christian lives, we can see how much of this self there is in each of us. It is so often self who tries to live the Christian life (the mere fact that we use the word "try" indicates that it is self who has the responsibility). It is self, too, who is often doing Christian work. It is always self who gets irritable and envious and resentful and critical and worried. It is self who is hard and unyielding in its attitudes to others. It is self who is shy and self-conscious and reserved. No wonder we need breaking. As long as self is in control, God can do little with us, for the fruit of the Spirit (enumerated in Galatians 5) with which God longs to fill us is the complete antithesis of the hard, unbroken spirit within us and presupposes that self has been crucified.

Being broken is both God's work and ours. He brings His pressure to bear, but we have to make the choice. If we are really open to conviction as we seek fellowship with God (and willingness for the light is the prime condition of fellowship with God), God will show us the expressions of this proud, hard self that cause Him pain. Then it is we can stiffen our necks and refuse to repent, or we can bow the head and say, "Yes, Lord." Brokenness in daily experience is simply the response of humility to the conviction of God. And inasmuch as this conviction is continuous, we shall need to be broken continually. And this can be very costly, when we see all the yielding of rights and selfish interests that this will involve, and the confessions and restitutions that may be sometimes necessary.

For this reason, we are not likely to be broken except at the cross of Jesus. The willingness of Jesus to be broken for us is the all-compelling motive in our being broken too. We see Him, who is in the form of God, counting not equality with God a prize to be grasped at and hung on to, but letting it go for us and taking upon Him the form of a Servant—God's Servant, man's Servant. We see Him willing to have no rights of His own, willing to let men revile Him and not revile again, willing to let men tread on Him and not retaliate or defend Himself. Above all, we see Him broken as He meekly goes to Calvary to become men's scapegoat by bearing their sins in His own body on the Tree. In a pathetic passage in a prophetic psalm, He says, "I am a worm, and no man."[2] Those who have been in tropical lands tell us that there is a big difference between a snake and a worm, when you attempt to strike at them. The snake rears itself up and hisses and tries to strike back—a true picture of self. But a worm offers no resistance, it allows you to do what you like with it, kick it or squash it under your heel—a picture of true brokenness. And Jesus was willing to become just that for us—a worm and no man. And He did so, because that is what He saw us to be, worms having forfeited all rights by our sin, except to deserve hell. And He now calls us to take our rightful place as worms for Him and with Him. The whole Sermon on the Mount with its teaching of non-retaliation, love for enemies and selfless giving, assumes that to be our position. But only the vision of the Love that was willing to be broken for us can constrain us to be willing for that.

---

[2] Psalm 22:6.

Lord, bend that proud and stiffnecked I,
  Help me to bow the head and die;
Beholding Him on Calvary,
  Who bowed His head for me.

But dying to self is not a thing we do once for all. There may be an initial dying when God first shows these things, but ever after it will be a constant dying, for only so can the Lord Jesus be revealed constantly through us.[3] All day long the choice will be before us in a thousand ways. It will mean no plans, no time, no money, no pleasure of our own. It will mean a constant yielding to those around us, for our yieldedness to God is measured by our yieldedness to man. Every humiliation, everyone who tries and vexes us, is God's way of breaking us, so that there is a yet deeper channel in us for the Life of Christ.

You see, the only life that pleases God and that can be victorious is His life—never our life, no matter how hard we try. But inasmuch as our self-centered life is the exact opposite of His, we can never be filled with His life unless we are prepared for God to bring our life constantly to death. And in that we must co-operate by our moral choice.

---

[3] 2 Cor. 4:10.

·2·

Cups Running Over

Brokenness, however, is but the beginning of revival. Revival itself is being absolutely filled to overflowing with the Holy Spirit, and that is victorious living. If we were asked this moment if we were filled with the Holy Spirit, how many of us would dare to answer "yes"? Revival is when we can say "yes" at any moment of the day. It is not egotistic to say so, for filling to overflowing is utterly and completely God's work—it is all of grace. All we have to do is to present our empty, broken self and let Him fill and keep filled. Andrew Murray says, "Just as water ever seeks and fills the lowest place, so the moment God finds you abased and empty, His glory and power flow in." The picture that has made things simple and clear to so many of us is that of the human heart as a cup, which we hold out to Jesus, longing that He might fill it with the Water of Life. Jesus is pictured as bearing the golden water pot with the Water of Life. As He passes by He looks into our cup, and if it is clean, He fills it to overflowing with the Water of Life. And as Jesus is always passing by, the cup can be always running over. That is something of what David meant, when he said, "My cup runneth over." This is revival—the constant peace of God ruling in our hearts because we are full to overflowing ourselves, and sharing it with others. People imagine that dying to self makes one miserable. But it is just the opposite. It is the refusal to die to self that makes one miserable. The more we know of death with Him, the more we shall know of His life in us, and so the more of real peace and joy. His life, too, will overflow through us to lost souls in a real concern for their salvation, and to our fellow Christians in a deep desire for their blessing.

Under the Blood

Only one thing prevents Jesus filling our cups as He passes by, and this is sin in one of its thousand forms. The Lord Jesus does not fill dirty cups. Anything that springs from self, however small it may be, is sin. Self-energy or self-complacency in service is sin. Self-pity in trials or difficulties, self-seeking in business or Christian work, self-indulgence in one's spare time, sensitiveness, touchiness, resentment and self-defense when we are hurt or injured by others, self-consciousness, reserve, worry, fear, all spring from self and all are sin and make our cups unclean.* But all of them were put into that other cup, which the Lord Jesus shrank from momentarily in Gethsemane, but which He drank to the dregs at Calvary—the cup of our sin. And if we will allow Him to show us what is in our cups and then give it to Him, He will cleanse them in the precious blood that still flows for sin. That does not mean mere cleansing from the guilt of sin, nor even from the stain of sin— though thank God both of these are true— but from the sin itself, whatever it may be. And as He cleanses our cups, so He fills them to overflowing with His Holy Spirit.

And we are able daily to avail ourselves of that precious blood. Suppose you have let the Lord Jesus cleanse your cup and have trusted

---

* Some may be inclined to question whether it is right to call such things as self-consciousness, reserve, and fear, sins. "Call them infirmities, disabilities, temperamental weaknesses, if you will," some have said, "but not sins. To do so would be to get us into bondage." The reverse, however, is true. If these things are not sins, then we must put up with them for the rest of our lives; there is no deliverance. But if these and other things like them are indeed sins, then there is a Fountain for sin, and we may experience cleansing and deliverance from them, if we put them immediately under His precious blood, the moment we are conscious of them. And they are sins. Their source is unbelief and an inverted form of pride, and they have hindered and hidden Him times without number.

Him to fill it to overflowing, then something comes along—a touch of envy or temper. What happens? Your cup becomes dirty and it ceases to overflow. And if we are constantly being defeated in this way, then our cup is never overflowing.

If we are to know continuous revival, we must learn the way to keep our cups clean. It is never God's will that a revival should cease, and be known in history as the revival of this or that year. When that happens it is due to only one thing—sin, just those little sins that the devil drops into our cup. But if we will go back to Calvary and learn afresh the power of the blood of Jesus to cleanse moment by moment from the beginnings of sin, then we have learned the secret of cups constantly cleansed and constantly overflowing. The moment you are conscious of that touch of envy, criticism, irritability, whatever it is— ask Jesus to cover it with His precious blood and cleanse it away and you will find the re- action gone, your joy and peace restored, and your cup running over. And the more you trust the blood of Jesus in this way, the less will you even have these reactions. But cleans- ing is only possible when we have first been broken before God on the point concerned. Suppose we are irritated by certain traits in someone. It is not enough just to take our re-actions of irritation to Calvary. We must first be broken; that is, we must yield to God over the whole question and accept that person and his ways as His will for us. Then we are able to take our wrong reaction to Jesus, knowing that His blood will cleanse away our sin; and when we have been cleansed from sin, let us not keep mourning over it, let us not be occupied with ourselves. But let us look up to our victorious Lord, and praise Him that He is still victorious.

There is one simple but all-inclusive guide the Word of God gives to regulate our walk with Jesus and to make us to know when sin has come in. Colossians 3:15 says, "Let the peace of God rule in your hearts." Everything that disturbs the peace of God in our hearts is sin, no matter how small it is, and no matter how little like sin it may at first appear to be. This peace is to "rule" our hearts, or (a more literal translation) "be the referee" in our hearts. When the referee blows his whistle at a football match, the game has to stop, a foul has been committed. When we lose our peace, God's referee in our hearts has blown his whistle! Let us stop immediately, ask God to show us what is wrong, put by faith the sin He shows us under the blood of Jesus, and then peace will be restored and we shall go on our way with our cups running over. If, however, God does not give us His peace, it will be because we are not really broken. Perhaps we have yet to say "sorry" to somebody else as well as to God. Or perhaps we still feel it is the other person's fault. But if we have lost our peace, it is obvious whose fault it is. We do not lose peace with God over another person's sin, but only over our own. God wants to show us our reactions, and only when we are willing to be cleansed there will we have His peace. Oh, what a simple but searching thing it is to be ruled by the peace of God, none other than the Holy Spirit Himself! Former selfish ways, which we never bothered about, are now shown to us and we cannot walk in them without the referee blowing his whistle. Grumbling, bossiness, carelessness, down to the smallest thing, are all revealed as sins when we are prepared to let our days be ruled by the peace of God. Many times a day and over the smallest things we shall have to avail ourselves of the cleansing blood of Jesus, and we shall find ourselves walking the way of brokenness as never before. But Jesus will be manifested in all His loveliness and grace in that brokenness.

Many of us, however, have neglected the referee's whistle so often and for so long that we have ceased to hear it. Days follow days and we feel we have little need of cleansing and no occasion of being broken. In that condition we are usually in a worse state than we ever imagine. It will take a great hunger for restored fellowship with God to possess our hearts before we will be willing to cry to God to show us where the blood of Jesus must be applied. He will show us, to begin with, just one thing, and it will be our obedience and brokenness on that one thing that will be the first step into revival for us.

·3·

The Way of Fellowship

When man fell and chose to make himself, rather than God, the center of his life, the effect was not only to put man out of fellowship with God, but also out of fellowship with his fellow man. The story of man's first quarrel with God in the third chapter of Genesis is closely followed, in the fourth chapter, by the story of man's first quarrel with his fellow—Cain's murder of Abel. The Fall is simply, "We have turned every one to his own way."[1] If I want my own way rather than God's, it is quite obvious that I shall want my own way rather than the other man's. A man does not assert his independence of God to surrender it to a fellow man, if he can help it. But a world in which each man wants his own way cannot but be a world full of tensions, barriers, suspicions, misunderstandings, clashes, and conflicts.

Now the work of the Lord Jesus Christ on the cross was not only to bring men back into

[1] Isa. 53:6.

fellowship with God, but also into fellowship with their fellow men. Indeed it cannot do one without the other. As the spokes get nearer the center of the wheel, they get nearer to one another. But if we have not been brought into vital fellowship with our brother, it is a proof that to that extent we have not been brought into vital fellowship with God. The First Epistle of John (what a new light revival sheds on this portion of Scripture!) insists on testing the depth and reality of a man's fellowship with God by the depth and reality of his fellowship with his brethren.[2] Some of us have come to see how utterly connected a man's relationship to his fellows is with his relationship to God. Everything that comes as a barrier between us and another, be it ever so small, comes as a barrier between us and God. We have found that where these barriers are not put right immediately, they get thicker and thicker until we find ourselves shut off from God and our brother by what seem to be veritable brick walls. Quite obviously, if we allow new life to come to us, it will have to manifest itself by a walk of oneness with God and our brother, with nothing between.

---

[2] 1 John 2:9; 3:14–15; 4:20.

Light and Darkness

On what basis can we have real fellowship with God and our brother? Here 1 John 1:7 has come afresh to us. *"If we walk in the light, as he is in the light, we have fellowship one with another, and the blood of Jesus Christ his Son cleanseth us from all sin."* What is meant by light and darkness is that light reveals, darkness hides. When anything reproves us, shows us up as we really are—that is light. "Whatsoever doth make manifest is light."[3] But whenever we do anything or say anything (or don't say anything) to hide what we are or what we've done—that is darkness.

Now the first effect of sin in our lives is always to make us try to hide what we are. Sin made our first parents hide behind the trees of the Garden and it has had the same effect on us ever since. Sin always involves us in being unreal, pretending, duplicity, window dressing, excusing ourselves and blaming others—and we can do all that as much by our silence as by saying or doing something. This is what the previous verse calls "walking in darkness." With some of us, the sin in question may be nothing more than self-consciousness (anything with "I" in it is sin) and the hiding, nothing more than an assumed

---

[3] Eph. 5:13.

heartiness to cover that self-consciousness; but it is walking in darkness nonetheless.

In contrast to all this in us, verse 5 of this chapter of 1 John tells us that "God is light," that is, God is the All-revealing One, who shows up every man as he really is. And it goes on to say, "In him is no darkness at all," that is, there is absolutely nothing in God which can be one with the tiniest bit of darkness or hiding in us.

Quite obviously, then, it is utterly impossible for us to be walking in any degree of darkness and have fellowship with God. While we are in that condition of darkness, we cannot have true fellowship with our brother either—for we are not real with him, and no one can have fellowship with an unreal person. A wall of reserve separates him and us.

The Only Basis for Fellowship

The only basis for real fellowship with God and man is to live out in the open with both. "But if we walk in the light, as he is in the light, we have fellowship one with another." To walk in the light is the opposite of walking in darkness. Spurgeon defines it in one of his sermons as "the willingness to know and be known." As far as God is concerned, this means that we are willing to know the whole truth about ourselves, we are open to conviction. We will bend the neck to the first twinges of conscience. Everything He shows us to be sin, we will deal with as sin—we will hide or excuse nothing. Such a walk in the light cannot but disclose sin increasingly in our lives, and we shall see things to be sin which we never thought to be such before. For that reason we might shrink from this walk, and be tempted to make for cover. But the verse goes on with the precious words, "and the blood of Jesus Christ his Son cleanseth us from all sin." Everything that the light of God shows up as sin we can confess and carry to the Fountain of Blood and it is gone, gone from God's sight and gone from our hearts. By the power of the precious blood we can be made more stainless than the driven snow; and thus continually abiding in the light and cleansed by the blood, we have fellowship with God.

But the fellowship promised us here is not only with God, but "one with another"; and that involves us in walking in the light with our brother too. In any case, we cannot be "in the open" with God and "in the dark" with him. This means that we must be as willing to know the truth about ourselves from our brother as to know it from God. We must be prepared for him to hold the light to us (and we must be willing to do the same service for him) and challenge us in love about anything he sees in our lives which is not the highest. We must be willing not only to know, but to be known by him for what we really are. That means we are not going to hide our inner selves from those with whom we ought to be in fellowship; we are not going to window-dress and put on appearances; nor are we going to whitewash and excuse ourselves. We are going to be honest about ourselves with them. We are willing to give up our spiritual privacy, pocket our pride, and risk our reputations for the sake of being open and transparent with our brethren in Christ. It means, too, that we are not going to cherish any wrong feeling in our hearts about another, but we are first going to claim deliverance from it from God and put it right with the one concerned. As we walk this way, we shall find that we shall have fellowship with one another at an altogether new level, and we shall not love one another less, but infinitely more.

No Bondage

Walking in the light is simply walking with

Jesus. Therefore there need be no bondage about it. We have not necessarily got to tell everybody everything about ourselves. The fundamental thing is our *attitude* of walking in the light, rather than the *act*. Are we willing to be in the open with our brother—and be so in word when God tells us to? That is the "armor of light"—true transparency. This may sometimes be humbling, but it will help us to a new reality with Christ, and to a new self-knowledge. We have become so used to the fact that God knows all about us that it does not seem to register with us, and we inevitably end by not knowing the truth about ourselves. But let a man begin to be absolutely honest about himself with but one other, as God guides him, and he will come to a knowledge of himself and his sins that he never had before, and he will begin to see more clearly than ever before where the redemption of Christ has got to be applied progressively to his life. This is the reason why James tells us to put ourselves under the discipline of "confessing our faults one to another."

In 1 John 1:7, of course, the purpose of "walking in the light" is that we might "have fellowship one with another." And what fellowship it is when we walk this way together!

Obviously, love will flow from one to another when each is prepared to be known as the repentant sinner he is at the cross of Jesus. When the barriers are down and the masks are off, God has a chance of making us really one. But there is also the added joy of knowing that in such a fellowship we are "safe." No fear now that others may be thinking thoughts about us or having reactions toward us which they are hiding from us. In a fellowship which is committed to walk in the light beneath the cross, we know that if there is any thought about us it will quickly be brought into the light, either in brokenness and confession (where there has been wrong and unlove), or else as a loving challenge, as something that we ought to know about ourselves.

It must not, however, be forgotten that our walk in the light is first and foremost with the Lord Jesus. It is with Him first that we must get things settled and it is His cleansing and victory that must first be obtained. Then when God guides us to open our hearts with others, we come to them with far more of a testimony than a confession (except where that is specifically due) and we praise God together.

Teams of Two for Revival

Jesus wants you to begin walking in the light with Him in a new way today. Join with one other—your Christian friend, the person you live with, your wife, your husband. Drop the mask. God has doubtless convicted you of one thing more than another that you have got to be honest with them about. Start there. Be a team of two to work for revival within your circle. As others are broken at the cross they will be added to your fellowship, as God leads. Get together from time to time for fellowship and to share your spiritual experience with real openness. In complete oneness pray together for others, and go out as a team with fresh testimony. God through such a fellowship will begin to work wondrously. As He saves and blesses others in this vital way, they can start to live and work as a fellowship too. As one billiard ball will move another billiard ball, so one group will set off another group, until the whole of our land is covered with new life from the risen Lord Jesus.

·4·

The Highway of Holiness

One of the things that we must learn if we are to live the victorious Christian life is its utter simplicity. How complicated we have made it! Great volumes are written, all sorts of technical phrases are used, we are told the secret lies in this, or that, and so on. But to most of us it is all so complicated that, although we know it in theory, we are unable to relate what we know to our practical daily living. In order to make the simple truths we have been considering even clearer, we want in this chapter to cast them all in picture form.

The Highway

An "over-all" picture of the life of victory which has come to many of us is that of the Highway in Isaiah 35: "And an highway shall be there, and a way, and it shall be called The way of holiness." The picture is that of a Highway built up from the surrounding morass, the world. Though the Highway is narrow and uphill, it is not beyond any of us to walk it, for "the wayfaring men, though fools, shall not err therein." Though there are many dangers if we get off the road, while we keep to the Highway there is safety, for "no lion shall be there, nor any ravenous beast shall go up thereon." Only one kind of person is barred from walking there and that is the unclean one. "The unclean shall not pass over it." This includes not only the sinner who does not know Christ as his Saviour, but the Christian who does and yet is walking in unconfessed and uncleansed sin.

The only way onto the Highway is up a small, dark, forbidding hill—the Hill of Calvary. It is the sort of hill we have to climb on our hands and knees—especially our knees. If we are content with our present Christian life, if we do not desire with a desperate hunger to get onto the Highway, we shall never get to our knees and thus never climb the hill. But if we are dissatisfied, if we are hungry, then we will find ourselves ascending. Don't hurry. Let God make you really hungry for the Highway; let Him really drive you to your knees in longing prayer. Mere sightseers won't get very far. "Ye shall . . . find me, when ye shall search for me with all your heart."

A Low Door

At the top of the hill, guarding the way to the Highway, stands so gaunt and grim . . . the cross. There it stands, the divider of time and the divider of men. At the foot of the cross is a low door, so low that to get through it one has to stoop and crawl through. It is the only entrance to the Highway. We must go through it if we would go any further on our way. This door is called the Door of the Broken Ones. Only the broken can enter the Highway. To be broken means to be "not I, but Christ." There is in every one of us a proud, stiff-necked "I." The stiff neck began in the Garden of Eden when Adam and Eve, who had always bowed their heads in surrender to God's will, stiffened their necks, struck out for independence, and tried to be "as gods." All the way through the Bible, God charges His people with the same stiff neck; and it manifests itself in us, too. We are hard and unyielding. We are sensitive and easily hurt. We get irritable, envious, and critical. We are resentful and unforgiving. We are self-indulgent—and how often that can lead to impurity! Every one of these things, and many more, spring from this proud self within. If it were not there and

Christ were in its place, we would not have these reactions. Before we can enter the Highway, God must bend and break that stiff-necked self, so that Christ reigns in its stead. To be broken means to have no rights before God and man. It does not mean merely surrendering my rights to Him but rather recognizing that I haven't any, except to deserve hell. It means just being nothing and having nothing that I call my own, neither time, money, possessions, nor position.

In order to break our wills to His, God brings us to the foot of the cross and there shows us what real brokenness is. We see those wounded hands and feet, that face of love crowned with thorns, and we see the complete brokenness of the One who said, "Not my will, but Thine be done," as He drank the bitter cup of our sin to its dregs. So the way to be broken is to look on Him and to realize it was our sin which nailed Him there. Then as we see the love and brokenness of the God who died in our place, our hearts will become strangely melted and we will want to be broken for Him and we shall pray,

> *Oh, to be saved from myself, dear Lord,*
> *Oh, to be lost in Thee,*
> *Oh, that it might be no more I,*
> *But Christ that lives in me.*

And some of us have found that there is no prayer that God is so swift to answer as the prayer that He might break us.

A Constant Choice

But do not let us imagine that we have to be broken only once as we go through the door. Ever after it will be a constant choice before us. God brings His pressure to bear on us, but we have to make the choice. If someone hurts and slights us, we immediately have the choice of accepting the slight as a means of grace to humble us lower or we can resist it and stiffen our necks again with all the disturbance of spirit that that is bound to bring. All the way through the day our brokenness will be tested, and it is no use our pretending we are broken before God if we are not broken in our attitude to those around us. God nearly always tests us through other people. There are no second causes for the Christian. God's will is made known in His providences, and His providences are so often others with their many demands on us. If you find yourself in a patch of unbrokenness, the only way is to go afresh to Calvary and see Christ broken for you and you will come away willing to be broken for Him.

Over the Door of the Broken Ones is sprinkled the precious blood of the Lord Jesus. As we bend to crawl through, the blood cleanses from all sin. For not only have we to bend to get through, but only the clean can walk the Highway. Maybe you have never known Jesus as your Saviour, maybe you have known Him for years, but in either case you are defiled by sin, the sins of pride, envy, resentment, impurity, etc. If you will give them all to Him who bore them on the cross, He will whisper to you again what He once said on the cross, "It is finished," and your heart will be cleansed whiter than snow.

The Gift of His Fullness

So we get onto the Highway. There it stretches before us, a narrow uphill road, bathed in light, leading towards the Heavenly Jerusalem. The embankment on either side slopes away into thick darkness. In fact, the darkness creeps right to the very edges of the Highway, but on the Highway itself all is light. Behind us is the cross, no longer dark and forbidding but radiant and glowing, and we no longer see Jesus stretched across its arms, but walking the Highway overflowing with resurrection life. In His hands He carries a pitcher with the Water of Life. He comes right up to us and asks us to hold out our hearts, and just as if we were handing Him a cup, we present to Him our empty hearts. He looks inside—a painful scrutiny—and where He sees we have allowed His blood to cleanse them, He fills them with the Water of Life. So we go on our way rejoicing and praising God and overflowing with His new life. This is revival. You and I full of the Holy Spirit all the time, loving others and concerned for their salvation. No struggling, no tarrying. Just simply giving Him each sin to cleanse in His precious blood and accepting from His hand the free gift of His fullness, and then allowing Him to do the work through us. As we walk along with Him, He is always there continually filling so that our cups continually overflow.

So the rest of our Christian life simply consists now of walking along the Highway, with hearts overflowing, bowing the neck to His will all the time, constantly trusting the blood to cleanse us and living in complete oneness with Jesus. There is nothing spectacular about this life, no emotional experiences to sigh after and wait for. It is merely the day-by-day living of the life the Lord intended us to live. This is real holiness.

Off the Highway

But we may, and sometimes do, slip off the Highway, for it is narrow. One little step aside and we are off the path and in darkness. It is always because of a failure in obedience somewhere or a failure to be weak enough to let God do all. Satan is always beside the road, shouting at us, but he cannot touch us. But we can yield to his voice by an act of will. This is the beginning of sin and slipping away from Jesus. Sometimes we find ourselves stiffening our necks to someone, sometimes to God Himself. Sometimes jealousy or resentment assails us. Immediately we are over the side, for nothing unclean can walk the Highway. Our cup is dirtied and ceases to overflow and we lose our peace with God. If we do not come back to the Highway at once, we shall go further down the side. We must get back. How? The first thing to do is to ask God to show what caused us to slip off; and He will, though it often takes Him time to make us see. Perhaps someone annoyed me, and I was irritated. God wants me to see that it was not the thing that the person did that matters, but my reaction to it. If I had been broken, I would not have been irritated. So, as I look longingly back to the Highway, I see the Lord Jesus again and I see what an ugly thing it is to get irritable and that Jesus died to save me from being irritable. As I crawl up again to the Highway on hands and knees, I come again to Him and His blood for cleansing. Jesus is waiting there to fill my cup to overflowing once again. Hallelujah! No matter where you leave the Highway, you will always find Him calling you to come back and be broken again, and always the blood will be there to cleanse and make you clean. This is the great secret of the Highway—knowing what to do with sin, when sin has come in. The secret is always to take sin to the cross, see there its sinfulness, and then put it under the blood and reckon it gone.

So the real test all along the Highway will be—are our cups running over? Have we the peace of God in our hearts? Have we love and concern for others? These things are the barometer of the Highway. If they are disturbed, then sin has crept in somewhere—self-pity, self-seeking, self-indulgence in thought or deed, sensitiveness, touchiness, self-defense, self-consciousness, shyness, reserve, worry, fear, and so on.

Our Walk with Others

An important thing about the Highway

which has not been mentioned yet is that we do not walk this Highway alone. Others walk it with us. There is, of course, the Lord Jesus. But there are other wayfarers, too, and the rule of the road is that fellowship with them is as important as fellowship with Jesus. Indeed, the two are intimately connected. Our relationship with our fellows and our relationship with God are so linked that we cannot disturb one without disturbing the other. Everything that comes between us and another, such as impatience, resentment, or envy, comes between us and God. These barriers are sometimes no more than veils—veils through which we can still, to some extent, see. But if not removed immediately, they thicken into blankets and then into brick walls, and we are shut off from both God and our fellows, shut in to ourselves. It is clear why these two relationships should be so linked. "God is love," that is, love for others, and the moment we fail in love towards another, we put ourselves out of fellowship with God—for God loves him, even if we don't.

But more than that, the effect of such sins is always to make us "walk in darkness"—that is, to cover up and hide what we really are or what we are really feeling. That is always the meaning of "darkness" in Scripture, for while the light reveals, the darkness hides. The first effect of sin in us is always to make us hide; with the result that we are pretending, we are wearing a mask, we are not real with either God or man. And, of course, neither God nor man can fellowship with an unreal person.

The way back into fellowship with the Lord Jesus will bring us again into fellowship with our brother, too. All unlove must be recognized as sin and given to the Lord Jesus for His blood to cover—and then it can be put right with our brother also. As we come back to the Lord Jesus like this, we shall find His love for our brother filling our hearts and wanting to express itself in our actions toward him and we shall walk in fellowship together again.

So this is the Highway life. It is no new, astounding doctrine. It is not something new for us to preach. It is quite unspectacular. It is just a life to live day by day in whatever circumstances the Lord has put us. It does not contradict what we may have read or heard about the Christian life. It just puts into simple pictorial language the great truths of sanctification. To start to live this life now will mean revival in our lives. To continue to live it will be revival continued. Revival is just you and

I walking along the Highway in complete oneness with the Lord Jesus and with one another, with cups continually cleansed and overflowing with the life and love of God.

·5·

The Dove and the Lamb

Victorious living and effective soul winning are not the product of our better selves and hard endeavors, but are simply the fruit of the Holy Spirit. We are not called upon to produce the fruit, but simply to bear it. It is all the time to be *His* fruit. Nothing is more important, then, than that we should be continuously filled with the Holy Spirit, or to keep to the metaphor, that the "trees of the Lord should be continuously full of sap"— His sap.

How this may be so for us is graphically illustrated by the record, in the first chapter of John, of how the Holy Spirit came upon the Lord Jesus at His baptism. John the Baptist had seen Jesus coming to him and had said of Him, "Behold the Lamb of God, which taketh away the sin of the world." Then as he baptized Him, he saw the heavens opened and the Spirit of God descending like a Dove and lighting upon Him.

The Humility of God

What a suggestive picture we have here—
the Dove descending upon the Lamb and
resting herself upon Him! The Lamb and the
Dove are surely the gentlest of all God's creatures. The Lamb speaks of meekness and submissiveness and the Dove speaks of peace
(what more peaceful sound than the cooing
of a dove on a summer day). Surely this
shows us that the heart of Deity is humility.
When the eternal God chose to reveal Himself in His Son, He gave Him the name of the
Lamb; and when it was necessary for the Holy
Spirit to come into the world, He was revealed under the emblem of the Dove. Is it
not obvious, then, that the reason why we
have to be humble in order to walk with God
is not merely because God is so big and we
so little, that humility befits such little creatures—but because God is so humble?

The main lesson of this incident is that the
Holy Spirit, as the Dove, could only come
upon and remain upon the Lord Jesus because He was the Lamb. Had the Lord Jesus
had any other disposition than that of the
Lamb—humility, submissiveness, and self-
surrender—the Dove could never have rested
on Him. Being herself so gentle, she would

have been frightened away had not Jesus been meek and lowly in heart.

Here, then, we have pictured for us the condition upon which the same Holy Spirit can come upon us and abide upon us. The Dove can only abide upon us as we are willing to be as the Lamb. How impossible that He should rest upon us while self is unbroken! The manifestations of the unbroken self are the direct opposite of the gentleness of the Dove. Read again in Galatians 5 the ninefold fruit of the Spirit ("love, joy, peace, long-suffering, gentleness, goodness, faithfulness, meekness, self-control") with which the Dove longs to fill us! Then contrast it with the ugly works of the flesh (the New Testament name for the unbroken self) in the same chapter. It is the contrast of the snarling wolf with the gentle dove!

The Disposition of the Lamb

How clear, then, that the Holy Spirit will only come upon us and remain upon us as we are willing to be as the Lamb on each point on which He will convict us! And nothing is so searching and humbling as to look at the Lamb on His way to Calvary for us and to be shown in how many points we have been unwilling to take the position of a lamb for Him.

Look at Him for a moment as the Lamb. He was the *simple Lamb.** A lamb is the simplest of God's creatures. It has no schemes or plans for helping itself—it exists in helplessness and simplicity. Jesus made Himself as nothing for us, and became the simple Lamb. He had no strength of His own or wisdom of His own, no schemes to get Himself out of difficulties, just simple dependence on the Father all the time. "The Son can do nothing of himself, but what he seeth the Father do." But we—how complicated we are! What schemes we have had of helping ourselves and of getting ourselves out of difficulties. What efforts of our own we have resorted to, to live the Christian life and to do God's works, as if we were something and could do something. The Dove had to take His flight (at least as far as the conscious blessing of His Presence was concerned) because we were not willing to be simple lambs.

---

* I owe the descriptions of the Lamb in this chapter (the simple Lamb, the shorn Lamb, the silent Lamb, the spotless Lamb, the substitute Lamb) to a moving address given by my friend, Mr. Marshal Shallis, one-time Secretary of the Evangelistic Society in London, England.

Willing to Be Shorn

Then He was the *shorn Lamb,* willing to be shorn of His rights, His reputation, and every human liberty that was due to Him, just as a lamb is shorn of its wool. He never resisted: A lamb never does. When He was reviled for our sakes, He reviled not again. When He suffered, He threatened not. He never said, "You cannot treat Me like that. Don't you know that I am the Son of God?" But we—ah, we! on how many occasions have we been unwilling to be shorn of that which was our right. We were not willing for His sake to lose what was our own. We insisted, too, that we should be treated with the respect due to our position. We resisted, and we fought. The Dove had to take His flight from us for we were not willing to be shorn lambs, and we were left without peace, hard and unloving.

He Answered Nothing

Then further, He was the *silent Lamb.* "As a sheep before her shearers is dumb, so he openeth not his mouth." Facing the calumnies of men, we read, "He answered nothing." He never defended Himself, nor explained Himself. But we have been anything but silent when others have said unkind or untrue things about us. Our voices have been loud in self-defense and self-vindication, and there has been anger in our voices. We have excused ourselves, when we should have admitted frankly our wrong. On every such occasion the Dove had to take His flight, and withdraw His peace and blessing from our hearts, because we were not willing to be the silent lamb.

No Grudges

He was also the *spotless Lamb*. Not only did nothing escape His lips, but there was nothing in His heart but love for those who had sent Him to the cross. There was no resentment towards them, no grudges, no bitterness. Even as they were putting the nails through His hands, He was murmuring, "I forgive you," and He asked His Father to forgive them too. He was willing to suffer it in meekness for us. But what resentment and bitterness have not we had in our hearts— toward this one and that one, and over so much less than what they did to Jesus. Each reaction left a stain on our hearts, and the Dove had to fly away because we were not willing to bear it and forgive it for Jesus' sake.

Return, O Dove!

These, then, are the acts and attitudes which drive the Holy Spirit from our lives, as far as present blessing is concerned, and they are all sin. Sin is the only thing that hinders the revival of His church. The question of all questions for us just now is, "How can the Dove return to our lives with His peace and power?" The answer is again just simply, "The Lamb of God," for He is not only the simple Lamb and the shorn Lamb and the silent Lamb and the spotless Lamb, but above everything else He is the *substitute Lamb.*

To the Jew the lamb that was offered to God was always a substitute lamb. Its meekness and submissiveness was only incidental to its main work, that of being slain for his sin and of its blood being sprinkled on the altar to atone for it. The humility of the Lord Jesus in becoming our Lamb was necessary only that He might become on the cross our Substitute, our Scapegoat, carrying our sins in His own body on the Tree, so that there might be forgiveness for our sins and cleansing from all their stains, when we repent of them. But inasmuch as there is no past or future with God, but all is present and timeless, there is a sense in which the suffering of the Lord Jesus for the sins of which we have not repented is present too. What a vision it is when we see these sins wounding and hurting Him now! May this solemn thought break our proud hearts in repentance! For it is only when we have seen these sins of ours in the heart of Jesus, so that we are broken and willing to repent of them and put them right, that the blood of the Lamb cleanses us from them and the Dove returns with peace and blessing to our hearts.

> *He humbled Himself to the manger,*
>   *And even to Calvary's tree;*
> *But I am so proud and unwilling*
>   *His humble disciple to be.*
>
> *He yielded His will to the Father,*
>   *And chose to abide in the Light;*
> *But I prefer wrestling to resting,*
>   *And try by myself to do right.*
>
> *Lord, break me, then cleanse me and fill me*
>   *And keep me abiding in Thee;*
> *That fellowship may be unbroken,*
>   *And Thy Name be hallowed in me.*

A saintly African Christian told a congregation once that, as he was climbing the hill to the meeting, he heard steps behind him. He turned and saw a man carrying a very heavy load up the hill on his back. He was full of sympathy for him and spoke to him. Then he noticed that His hands were scarred, and he realized that it was Jesus. He said to Him, "Lord, are you carrying the world's sins up the hill?" "No," said the Lord Jesus, "not the *world's* sin, just yours!" As that African simply told the vision God had just given him, the people's hearts and his heart were broken as they saw their sins at the cross. Our hearts need to be broken too, and only when they are shall we be willing for the confessions, the apologies, the reconciliations and the restitutions that are involved in a true repentance of sin. Then, when we have been willing to humble ourselves, as the Lord humbled Himself, the Dove will return to us.

> *Return, O heavenly Dove, return,*
> *Sweet messenger of rest!*
> *I hate the sins that made Thee mourn,*
> *And drove Thee from my breast.*

Ruled by the Dove

One last word. The Dove is the emblem of peace, which suggests that if the blood of Jesus has cleansed us and we are walking with the Lamb in humility, the sign of the Spirit's presence and fullness will be peace. This is indeed to be the test of our walk all the way along. "Let the peace of God rule [arbitrate] in your hearts" (Col. 3:15). If the Dove ceases to sing in our hearts at any time, if our peace is broken, then it can only be because of sin. In some matter we have departed from the humility of the Lamb. We must ask God to show us what it is, and be quick to repent of it and bring the sin to the cross. Then the Dove will be once again in His rightful place in our hearts and peace with God will be ours. In this way we shall know that continuous abiding of the Spirit's presence which is open even to fallen men through the immediate and constant application of the precious blood of Jesus.

Shall we not begin from today to allow our lives to be ruled by the Heavenly Dove, the peace of God, and allow Him to be the arbiter all the day through? We shall find ourselves walking in a path of constant conviction and much humbling, but in this way we shall come into real conformity with the Lamb of God, and we shall know the only victory that is worth anything, the conquest of self.

·6·

Revival in the Home

Thousands of years ago, in the most beautiful garden the world has ever known, lived a man and a woman. Formed in the likeness of their Creator, they lived solely to reveal Him to His creation and to each other and thus to glorify Him every moment of the day. Humbly they accepted the position of a creature with the Creator—that of complete submission and yieldedness to His will. Because they always submitted their wills to His, because they lived for Him and not for themselves, they were also completely submitted to each other. Thus in that first home in that beautiful garden there was absolute harmony, peace, love, and oneness, not only with God but with each other.

Then one day the harmony was shattered, for the serpent stole into the God-centered home, and with him, sin. And now, because they had lost their peace and fellowship with God, they lost it with each other. No longer did they live for God—each lived for himself. They were each their own god now, and because they no longer lived for God they no longer lived for each other. Instead of peace, harmony, love, and oneness, there was now discord and hate—in other words, SIN!

Revival Begins at Home

It was into the home that sin first came. It is in the home that revival first needs to come. Revival is desperately needed in the church . . . in the country . . . in the world; but a revived church with unrevived homes would be sheer hypocrisy. It is the hardest place, the most costly, but the most necessary place to begin.

But before we go on, let us remind ourselves again of what revival really is. It simply means a new life in hearts where the spiritual life has ebbed—but not a new life of self-effort or self-initiated activity. It is not man's life, but God's life, the life of Jesus filling us and flowing through us. That life is manifested in fellowship and oneness with those with whom we live—nothing between us and God, and nothing between us and others. The home is the place before all others where this should be experienced.

But how different is the experience of so many of us professing Christians in our homes—little irritations, frayed tempers, selfishness and resentments; and even where there is nothing very definitely wrong between us, just not that complete oneness and fellowship that ought to characterize Christians living together. All the things that come between us and others come between us and God and spoil our fellowship with Him, so that our hearts are not overflowing with divine life.

What Is Wrong with Our Homes?

Now what at bottom is wrong with our homes? When we talk about homes, we mean the relationship which exists between a husband and wife, a parent and child, a brother and sister, or between any others who, through various circumstances, are compelled to live together.

The first thing that is wrong with so many families is that they are not really open with one another. We live so largely behind drawn blinds. The others do not know us for what we really are, and we do not intend that they should. Even those living in the most intimate relationships with us do not know what goes on inside—our difficulties, battles, failures, or what the Lord Jesus has to cleanse us from so frequently. This lack of transparency and openness is ever the result of sin. The first effect of the first sin was to make Adam and Eve hide from God behind the trees of the Garden. They who had been so transparent with God and with one another were then hiding from God, because of sin; and if they hid from God you can be quite sure that they soon began to hide from one another. There were reactions and thoughts in Adam's heart that Eve was never allowed to know and there were like things hidden in Eve's heart too. And so it has been ever since. Having something to hide from God, we hide it, too, from one another. Behind that wall of reserve, which acts like a mask, we cover our real selves. Sometimes we hide in the most extraordinary way behind an assumed jocular manner. We are afraid to be serious because we do not want others to get too close and see us as we really are, and so we keep up a game of bluff. We are not real with one another, and no one can have fellowship with an unreal person, and so oneness and close fellowship are impossible in the home. This is what the Scripture calls "walking in darkness"—for the darkness is anything which hides.

The Failure to Love

The second thing that is wrong with our homes is our failure really to love one another. "Well," says somebody, "that could never be said of our home, for no one could love one another more than my husband and I love each other!" But wait a minute! It depends on what you mean by love. Love is not just a sentimental feeling, nor even strong passion. The famous passage in 1 Corinthians 13 tells us what real love is, and if we test ourselves by it we may find that after all we are hardly loving one another at all, and our behavior is all in the opposite direction—and the opposite of love is hate! Let us look at some of the things that the passage tells us about love.

Love is longsuffering [*patient*] and is kind.

Love vaunteth not itself [*does not boast*], is not puffed up [*is not conceited*].

Love does not behave itself unseemly [*is not rude*], seeketh not her own [*is not selfish*], is not easily provoked [*does not get irritated*], thinketh no evil [*does not entertain unkind thoughts of another*].

How do we stand up to those tests in our

homes? So often we act in the very opposite way.

We are often impatient with one another and even unkind in the way we answer back or react.

How much envy, too, there can be in a home. A husband and wife can envy the other his gifts, even his spiritual progress. Parents may be envious of their children, and how often is there not bitter envy between brothers and sisters.

Also "not behaving unseemly," that is, courtesy, what about that? Courtesy is just love in little things, but it is in the little things that we trip up. We think we can "let up" at home.

How "puffed up," that is, conceited, we so often are! Conceit comes out in all sorts of ways. We think we know best, we want our way, and we nag or boss the other one; and nagging or bossing leads on to the tendency to despise the other one. Our very attitude of superiority sets us up above him. Then, when at the bottom of our hearts we despise someone, we blame him for everything—and yet we think we love.

Then what about "seeking not our own," that is, not being selfish? Many times a day we put our wishes and interests before those of the other one.

How "easily provoked" we are! How quick to be irritated by something in the other! How often we allow the unkind thought, the resentful feeling over something the other has done or left undone!—yet we profess there are no failures in love in our homes. These things happen every day and we think nothing of them. They are all of them the opposite of love, and the opposite of love is hate. Impatience is hate, envy is hate, conceit and self-will are hate, and so are selfishness, irritability, and resentment! And hate is SIN. "He that saith he is in the light, and hateth his brother, is in darkness even until now." What tensions, barriers, and discord it all causes, and fellowship with both God and the other is made impossible.

The Only Way Out

Now the question is, Do I want new life, revival, in my home? I have got to challenge my heart about this. Am I prepared to continue in my present state, or am I really hungry for new life, His life, in my home? For not unless I am really hungry will I be willing to take the necessary steps. The first step I must take is to call sin *sin* (my sin, not the other person's), and go with it to the cross, and trust the Lord Jesus there and then to cleanse me from it.

As we bow the neck at the cross, His self-forgetful love for others, His longsuffering and forbearance flow into our hearts. The precious blood cleanses us from the unlove and ill will and the Holy Spirit fills us with the very nature of Jesus. 1 Corinthians 13 is nothing less than the nature of Jesus, and it is all gift to us, for His nature *is* ours, if He is ours. This blessed process can happen every single time the beginnings of sin and unlove creep in, for the cleansing Fountain of Blood is available to us all the time.

All this will commit us very definitely to walking the Way of the Cross in our homes. Again and again we will see places where we must yield up our rights, as Jesus yielded up His for us. We shall have to see that the thing in us that reacts so sharply to another's selfishness and pride is simply our own selfishness and pride, which we are unwilling to sacrifice. We shall have to accept another's ways and doings as God's will for us and meekly bend the neck to all God's providences. That does not mean that we must accept another's selfishness as God's will for *him*—far from it—but only as God's will for *us*. As far as the other is concerned, God will probably want to use us, if we are broken, to help him see his need. Certainly, if we are parents we shall often need to correct our child with firmness. But none of this is to be from selfish motives, but only out of love for the other and a longing for his good. Our own convenience and rights must all the time be yielded. Only so will the love of the Lord Jesus be able to fill us and express itself through us.

When we have been broken at Calvary we must be willing to put things right with others—sometimes even with the children. This is, so often, the test of our brokenness. Brokenness is the opposite of hardness. Hardness says, "It's your fault!" Brokenness, however, says, "It's my fault." What a different atmosphere will begin to prevail in our homes when they hear us say that!

Let us remember that at the cross there is room for only one at a time. We cannot say, "I was wrong, but you were wrong too. You must come as well!" No, you must go alone, saying, "I'm wrong." God will work in the other more through your brokenness than through anything else you can do or say. We may, however, have to wait—perhaps a long time. But that should only cause us to understand more perfectly how God feels, for, as someone has said, "He too has had to wait a long time since His great attempt to put things right with man nineteen hundred years ago, although there was no wrong on His side." But God will surely answer our prayer and bring the other to Calvary too. There we shall be one; there the middle wall of partition between us will be broken down; there we shall be able to walk in the light, in true transparency, with Jesus and with one another, loving each other with a pure heart fervently.

Sin is almost the only thing we have in common with everyone else, and so at the feet of Jesus where sin is cleansed is the only place where we can be one. Real oneness conjures up for us the picture of two or more sinners together at Calvary.

·7·

The Mote and the Beam

That friend of ours has got something in his eye! Though it is only something tiny—what Jesus called a mote—how painful it is and how helpless he is until it is removed! It is surely our part as a friend to do all we can to remove it, and how grateful he is to us when we have succeeded in doing so. We would be equally grateful to him if he did the same service for us.

In the light of that, it seems clear that the real point of the well-known passage in Matthew 7:3–5 about the beam and the mote is not the forbidding of our trying to remove the fault in the other person, but rather the reverse. It is the injunction that at all costs we should do this service for one another. True, its first emphasis seems to be a condemnation of censoriousness, but when the censoriousness in us is removed, the passage ends by saying, "Then shalt thou see clearly to cast the mote out of thy brother's eye." According to the New Testament, we are meant to care so much for the other man that we are willing to do all we can to remove from his eye the mote which is marring his vision and hindering his blessing. We are told to "admonish one another" and "exhort one another," to "wash one another's feet" and to "provoke one another to love and good works." The love of Jesus poured out in us will make us want to help our brother in this way.

What blessing may not come to many others through our willingness humbly to challenge one another, as led by God. A humble Swiss, named Nicholas of Basle, one of the Society of the "Friends of God," crossed the mountains to Strassburg and entered the church of Dr. Tauler, the popular preacher of that city. Said Nicholas, "Dr. Tauler, before you can do your greatest work for God, the world and this city, you must die—die to yourself, your gifts, your popularity, and even your own goodness, and when you have learned the full meaning of the cross, you will have a new power with God and man." That humble challenge from an obscure Christian changed Dr. Tauler's life, and he did indeed learn to die, and became one of the great factors to prepare the way for Luther and the

Reformation. In this passage the Lord Jesus tells us how we may do this service for one another.

What Is the Beam?

First, however, the Lord Jesus tells us that it is only too possible to try to take the tiny mote, a tiny speck of sawdust, out of the other's eye when there is a beam, a great length of timber, in ours. When that is the case, we haven't a chance of casting out the mote in the other, because we cannot see straight ourselves, and in any case it is sheer hypocrisy to attempt to do so.

Now we all know what Jesus meant by the mote in the other person's eye. It is some fault which we fancy we can discern in him; it may be an act he has done against us, or some attitude he adopts towards us. But what did the Lord Jesus mean by the beam in our eye? I suggest that the beam in our eye is simply our unloving reaction to the other man's mote. Without doubt there is a wrong in the other person. But our reaction to that wrong is wrong too! The mote in him has provoked in us resentment, or coldness, or criticism, or bitterness, or evil speaking, or ill will—all of them variants of the basic ill, unlove. And that, says the Lord Jesus, is far, far worse than the tiny wrong (sometimes quite unconscious) that provoked it. A mote means in the Greek a little splinter, whereas a beam means a rafter. And the Lord Jesus means by this comparison to tell us that our unloving reaction to the other's wrong is what a great rafter is to a little splinter! Every time we point one of our fingers at another and say, "It's your fault," three of our fingers are pointing back at us. God have mercy on us for the many times when it has been so with us and when in our hypocrisy we have tried to deal with the person's fault, when God saw there was this thing far worse in our own hearts.

But let us not think that a beam is of necessity some *violent* reaction on our part. The first beginning of a resentment is a beam, as is also the first flicker of an unkind thought, or the first suggestion of unloving criticism. Where that is so, it only distorts our vision and we shall never see our brother as he really is, beloved of God. If we speak to our brother with that in our hearts, it will only provoke him to adopt the same hard attitude to us, for it is a law of human relationships that "with what measure ye mete, it shall be measured to you again."

Take It to Calvary

No! "First cast out the beam out of thine own eye." That is the first thing we must do. We must recognize our unloving reaction to him as sin. On our knees we must go with it to Calvary and see Jesus there and get a glimpse of what that sin cost Him. At His feet we must repent of it and be broken afresh and trust the Lord Jesus to cleanse it away in His precious blood and fill us with His love for that one—and He will, and does, if we will claim His promise. Then we shall probably need to go to the other in the attitude of the repentant one, tell him of the sin that has been in our heart and what the blood has effected there and ask him to forgive us too. Very often bystanders will tell us, and sometimes our own hearts, that the sin we are confessing is not nearly as bad as the other's wrong, which he is not yet confessing. But we have been to Calvary; indeed, we are learning to live under the shadow of Calvary; and we have seen our sin there and we can no longer compare our sin with another's. But as we take these simple steps of repentance, then we see clearly to cast the mote out of the other's eye, for the beam in our eye has gone. In that moment God will pour light in on us as to the other's need, that neither he nor we ever had before. We may see then that the mote we were so conscious of before is virtually non-existent—it was but the projection of something that was in us. On the other hand, we may have revealed to us hidden underlying things of which our brother was hardly conscious. Then as God leads us, we must lovingly and humbly challenge him, so that he may see them too, and bring them to the fountain for sin and find deliverance. He will be more likely than ever to let us do it—indeed, if he is a humble man he will be grateful to us, for he will know now that there is no selfish motive in our heart, but only love and concern for him.

When God is leading us to challenge another, let not fear hold us back. Let us not argue or press our point. Let us just say what God has told us to and leave it there. It is God's work, not ours, to cause the other to see it. It takes time to be willing to bend "the proud stiff-necked I." When we in turn are challenged, let us not defend ourselves and explain ourselves. Let us take it in silence, thanking the other; and then go to God about it and ask Him. If he was right, let us be humble enough to go and tell him, and praise God together. There is no doubt that we need each other desperately. There are blind spots in all our lives that we shall never see unless we are prepared for another to be God's channel to us.

·8·

Are You Willing to Be a Servant?

Nothing is clearer from the New Testament than that the Lord Jesus expects us to take the low position of servants. This is not just an extra obligation, which we may or may not assume as we please. It is the very heart of that new relationship which the disciple is to take up with respect to God and to his fellows if he is to know fellowship with Christ and any degree of holiness in his life. When we understand the humbling and self-emptying that is involved in really being a servant, it becomes evident that only those who are prepared to live quite definitely under the shadow of Calvary, ever contemplating the humility and brokenness of the Lord Jesus for us, will be willing for that position.

As we approach this subject and its personal application in detail to our lives, there are three preliminary things which need to be said to prepare us to understand the low and humbling position which He wants us to take.

In the Old Testament two sorts of servants
are mentioned. There are the *hired servants*,
who have wages paid to them and have certain rights. Then there are the *bond servants*,
or slaves, who have no rights, who receive
no wages, and who have no appeal. The He-
brews were forbidden ever to make bond servants of their own race. Only of the Gentiles
were they permitted to take such slaves.
When, however, we come to the New Testament, the word in the Greek for the servant
of the Lord Jesus Christ is not "hired servant"
but "bond servant," by which is meant to be
shown that our position is one where we have
no rights and no appeal, where we are the
absolute property of our Master, to be treated
and disposed of just as He wishes.

Further, we shall see more clearly still what
our position is to be when we understand that
we are to be the bond servants of One who
was Himself willing to be a bond servant.
Nothing shows better the amazing humility
of the Lord Jesus, whose servants we are to
be, than that though He was in the form of
God, He "counted it not a prize to be on an
equality with God, but emptied himself, taking the form of a servant" (Phil. 2:6–7, ERV)
—without rights, willing to be treated as the

will of the Father and the malice of men might decree, if only He might thereby serve men and bring them back to God. And you and I are to be the bond servants of Him who was and always is a bond servant, whose disposition is ever that of humility and whose activity is ever that of humbling Himself to serve His creatures. How utterly low, then, is our true position! How this shows us what it means to be ruled by the Lord Jesus!

That leads us to something further. Our servanthood to the Lord Jesus is to express itself in our servanthood to our fellows. Says Paul, "We preach not ourselves, but Christ Jesus the Lord; and ourselves your servants for Jesus' sake." The low position we take toward the Lord Jesus is judged by Him by the low position we take in our relationship with our fellows. An unwillingness to serve others in costly, humbling ways He takes to be an unwillingness to serve Him, and we thus put ourselves out of fellowship with Him.

We are now in a position to apply all this much more personally to our lives. God spoke to me some time ago through Luke 17:7–10: "But which of you, having a servant plowing or feeding cattle, will say unto him by and by, when he is come from the field, Go and sit down to meat? And will not rather say unto him, Make ready wherewith I may sup, and gird thyself, and serve me, till I have eaten and drunken; and afterward thou shalt eat and drink? Doth he thank that servant because he did the things that were commanded him? I trow not. So likewise ye, when ye shall have done all those things which are commanded you, say, We are unprofitable servants: we have done that which was our duty to do."

I see here five marks of the bond servant. *First of all, he must be willing to have one thing on top of another put upon him, without any consideration being given him.* On top of a hard day in the field the servant in the parable had immediately to prepare his master's meal, and on top of that he had to wait at table—and all that before he had had any food himself. He just went and did it, expecting nothing else. How unwilling we are for this! How quickly there are murmurings and bitterness in our hearts when that sort of thing is expected of us. But the moment we start murmuring, we are acting as if we had rights, and a bond servant hasn't any!

Secondly, in doing this he must be willing not to be thanked for it. How often we serve others, but what self-pity we have in our hearts and how bitterly we complain that they take it as a matter of course and do not thank us for it. But a bond servant must be willing for that. Hired servants may expect something, but not bond servants.

And, thirdly, having done all this, he must not charge the other with selfishness. As I read the passage, I could not but feel that the master was rather selfish and inconsiderate. But there is no such charge from the bond servant. He exists to serve the interests of his master, and the selfishness or otherwise of his master does not come into it with him. But we? We can perhaps allow ourselves to be "put upon" by others, and are willing perhaps not to be thanked for what we do, but how we charge the other in our minds with selfishness! But that is not the place of a bond servant. He is to find in the selfishness of others but a further opportunity to identify himself afresh with his Lord as the servant of all.

But there is a *fourth* step still to which we must go. Having done all that, there is no ground for pride or self-congratulation, *but we must confess that we are unprofitable servants,* that is, that we are of no real use to God or man in ourselves. We must confess again and again that "in us, that is in our flesh, there dwelleth no good thing," that, if we have acted thus, it is no thanks to us, whose hearts are naturally proud and stubborn, but only to the Lord Jesus, who dwells in us and who has made us willing.

The bottom of self is quite knocked out by the *fifth* and last step—*the admission that doing and bearing what we have in the way of meekness and humility, we have not done one stitch more than it was our duty to do.* God made man in the first place simply that he might be God's bond servant. Man's sin has simply consisted in his refusal to be God's bond servant. His restoration can only be, then, a restoration to the position of a bond servant. A man, then, has not done anything specially meritorious when he has consented to take that position, for he was created and redeemed for that very thing.

This, then, is the Way of the Cross. It is the way that God's lowly Bond Servant first trod for us, and should not we, the bond servants of that Bond Servant, tread it still? Does it seem hard and forbidding, this way down? Be assured, it is the only way up. It was the way by which the Lord Jesus reached the throne, and it is the way by which we too reach the place of spiritual power, authority, and fruitfulness. Those who tread this path are radiant, happy souls, overflowing with the life of their Lord. They have found "he that humbleth himself shall be exalted" to be true for them as for their Lord. Where before humility was an unwelcome intruder to be put up with only on occasion, she has now become the spouse of their souls, to whom they have wedded themselves forever. If darkness and unrest enter their souls it is only because somewhere on some point they have been unwilling to walk with her in the paths of meekness and brokenness. But she is ever ready to welcome them back into her company, as they seek her face in repentance.

That brings us to the all-important matter of repentance. We shall not enter into more abundant life merely by resolving that we shall be humbler in the future. There are attitudes and actions which have already taken place and are still being persisted in (if only by our unwillingness to apologize for them) that must first be repented of. The Lord Jesus did not take upon Him the form of a bond servant merely to give us an example, but that He might die for these very sins upon the cross, and open a fountain where in His precious blood they can all be washed away. But that blood cannot be applied to the sins of our proud hearts until we have been broken in repentance as to what has already happened and as to what we already are. This will mean allowing the light of God to go through every part of our hearts and into every one of our relationships. It will mean that we shall have to see that the sins of pride, which God will show us, made it necessary for Jesus to come from heaven and die on the cross that they might be forgiven. It will mean not only asking Him to forgive us but asking others too. And that will be humbling indeed. But as we crawl through the Door of the Broken Ones we shall emerge into the light and glory of the highway of holiness and humility.

· 9 ·

The Power of
the Blood of the Lamb

The message and challenge of revival, which is coming to many of us these days, is searching in its utter simplicity. It is simply that there is only one thing in the world that can hinder the Christian's walking in victorious fellowship with God and his being filled with the Holy Spirit—and that is sin in one form or another. There is only one thing in the world that can cleanse him from sin with all that that means of liberty and victory—and that is the power of the blood of the Lord Jesus. It is, however, most important for us that we should see what it is that gives the blood of Christ its mighty power with God on behalf of men, for then we shall understand the conditions on which its full power may be experienced in our lives.

How many achievements and how many blessings for men the Scripture ascribes to the power of the blood of the Lord Jesus! By the power of His blood peace is made between man and God.[1] By its power there is forgiveness of sins and eternal life for all who put their faith in the Lord Jesus.[2] By the power of His blood Satan is overcome.[3] By its power there is continual cleansing from all sin for us.[4] By the power of His blood we may be set free from the tyranny of an evil conscience to serve the living God.[5] By its infinite power with God the most unworthy have liberty to enter the Holy of Holies of God's presence and live there all the day.[6] We may well ask what gives the blood its power!

To that question we need to link this other question: How may we experience its full power in our lives? Too often that precious blood does not have its cleansing, peace-giving, life-giving, sin-destroying power in our hearts, and too often we do not find ourselves in God's presence and fellowship all the day.

Whence Its Power?

The answer to the first question is suggested by the phrase in the book of Revelation which describes the blood of Christ by the tender expression "the blood of the Lamb."[7] Not the blood of the *Warrior*, but the

---

[1] Col. 1:20. [2] Col. 1:14; John 6:54. [3] Rev. 12:11. [4] 1 John 1:7. [5] Heb. 9:14.
[6] Heb. 10:19. [7] Rev. 7:14.

blood of the *Lamb*! In other words, that which gives the precious blood its power with God for men is the lamb-like disposition of the One who shed it and of which it is the supreme expression. The title "the Lamb" so frequently given to the Lord Jesus in Scripture is first of all descriptive of His work—that of being a sacrifice for our sin. When a sinning Israelite wanted to get right with God, it was the blood of a lamb (sometimes that of a goat) which had to be shed and sprinkled on the altar. Jesus is the divine fulfillment of all those lambs that men offered—the Lamb of God who takes away the sin of the world.[8] But the title "the Lamb" has a deeper meaning. It describes His character. He is the Lamb in that He is meek and lowly in heart,[9] gentle and unresisting, and all the time surrendering His own will to the Father's,[10] for the blessing and saving of men. Anyone but the Lamb would have resented and resisted the treatment men gave Him. But He, in obedience to the Father[11] and out of love for us, did neither. Men did what they liked to Him and for our sakes He yielded all the time. When He was reviled, He reviled not again. When He suffered, He threatened not. No standing up for His rights, no hitting back, no resentment, no complain-

---

[8] John 1:29.   [9] Matt. 11:29.   [10] John 6:38.   [11] Phil. 2:8.

ing! How different from us! When the
Father's will and the malice of men pointed
to dark Calvary, the Lamb meekly bowed His
head in willingness for that too. It was as the
Lamb that Isaiah saw Him, when he proph-
esied, "He is brought as a lamb to the slaugh-
ter, and as a sheep before her shearers is
dumb, so he openeth not his mouth."[12] The
scourging, the scoffing, the spitting, the hair
plucked off from His cheeks, the weary last
march up the Hill, the nailing and the lifting
up, the piercing of His side and the flowing
of His blood—none of these things would
ever have been, had He not been the Lamb.
And all that to pay the price of *my* sin! So we
see not merely is He the Lamb because He
died on the cross, but He died upon the cross
because He is the Lamb.

Let us ever see this disposition in the blood.
Let every mention of the blood call to mind
the deep humility and self-surrender of the
Lamb, for it is this disposition that gives the
blood its wonderful power with God. He-
brews 9:14 forever links the blood of Christ
with His self-offering to God: "How much
more shall the blood of Christ, who through
the eternal Spirit *offered himself* without spot
to God. . . ." And it is this fact that bestows
upon it its power with God for men. For this

---

[12] Isa. 53:7.

disposition has ever been of supreme value to God. Humility, lamb-likeness, the surrender of our wills to God, are what He looks for supremely from man. It was to manifest all this that God ever created the first man. It was his refusal to walk this path that constituted his first sin (and it has been the heart of sin ever since). It was to bring this disposition back to earth that Jesus came. It was simply because the Father saw this in Him that He could say, "My Son, in whom I am well pleased." It was because the shedding of His blood so supremely expressed this disposition that it is so utterly precious to God and so all-availing for man and his sin.

The Second Question

We come now to the second question: How can we experience its full power in our lives? Our hearts surely tell us the answer, as we look on the Lamb, bowing His head for us on Calvary—only by being willing to have the same disposition that ruled Him and by bending our necks in brokenness as He bowed His. Just as it is the disposition of the Lamb that bestows upon the blood its power, so it is only as we are willing to be partakers of the same disposition of the Lamb that we shall know its full power in our lives. And we may be partakers of His disposition,[13] for it has been made transferable to us by His death. All the fruits of the Holy Spirit, mentioned in Galatians 5—love, joy, peace, longsuffering, gentleness, goodness, faith, meekness, self-control—what are they but the expressions of the lamb-like nature of the Lord Jesus with which the Holy Spirit wants to fill us? Let us never forget that the Lord Jesus, though exalted to the throne of God, is still the Lamb (the book of Revelation tells us that) and He wants to reproduce Himself in us.

Are We Willing?

But are we willing for this? There is a hard, unyielding self, which stands up for itself and resists others, that will have to be broken if we are to be willing for the disposition of the Lamb, and if the precious blood is to reach us in cleansing power. We may pray long to be cleansed from some sin and for peace to be restored to our hearts, but unless we are willing to be broken on the point in question and be made a partaker of the Lamb's humility there, nothing will happen. Every sin we ever commit is the result of the hard, unbroken self taking up some attitude of pride, and

---

[13] Phil. 2:5; 1 Cor. 2:16.

we shall not find peace through the blood until we are willing to see the source of each sin and reverse the wrong attitude that caused it by a specific repentance, which will always be humbling. This does not mean that we need to try to make ourselves feel the humility of Jesus; for we have only to walk in the light and be willing for God to reveal any sin that may be in our lives and we shall find ourselves asked by the Lord to perform all sorts of costly acts of repentance and surrender, often over what we term small and trivial matters. But their importance can be gauged by what it costs our pride to put them right. He may show us a confession or apology that has to be made to someone or an act of restitution that has to be done.[14] He may show us that we must give in on something and yield up our fancied rights in it (Jesus had no rights—have we then?). He may show us that we must go to the one who has done us a wrong and confess to him the far greater wrong of resenting it (Jesus never resented anything or anyone—have we any right to?). He may call us to be open with our friends that they may know us as we really are, and thus be able to have true fellowship with us. These acts may well be humiliating and a complete reversal of our usual attitudes of

---

[14] Matt. 5:23–24.

pride and selfishness, but by such acts we shall know true brokenness and become partakers of the humility of the Lamb.[15] As we are willing for this in each issue, the blood of the Lamb will be able to cleanse us from all sin and we shall walk with God in white, with His peace in our hearts.

---

[15] 2 Cor. 4:10.

· 10 ·

Protesting Our Innocence?

We have all become so used to condemning the proud self-righteous attitude of the Pharisee in the parable of the Pharisee and the Publican[1] that we can hardly believe that the picture of him there is meant to apply to us—which only shows how much like him we really are. The Sunday School teacher was never so much a Pharisee as when she finished her lesson on this parable with the words, "And now, children, we can thank God that we are not as this Pharisee!" In particular we are in danger of adopting the Pharisee's attitude when God is wanting to humble us at the cross of Jesus, and show us the sins in our hearts that are hindering personal revival.

God's Picture of the Human Heart

We shall not understand the real wrong of the Pharisee's attitude, nor of our own, un-

---

[1] Luke 18:9–14.

less we view it against the background of
what God says about the human heart. Said
Jesus Christ, "From within, out of the heart
of men, proceed evil thoughts, adulteries, for-
nications, murders, thefts, covetousness,
wickedness, deceit, lasciviousness, an evil
eye, blasphemy, pride, foolishness."[2] The
same dark picture of the human heart is given
us in Paul's letter to the Galatians: "The works
of the flesh are manifest, which are these:
adultery, fornication, uncleanness, lasciviousness, idolatry, witchcraft, hatred, variance,
emulations, wrath, strife, seditions, heresies,
envyings, murders, drunkenness, revellings,
and such like."[3] What a picture! Jeremiah
adds the same witness: "The heart is deceit-
ful above all things [that is, it deceives the
man himself, so that he does not know him-
self] and desperately wicked: who can know
it?"[4] Here then is God's picture of the human
heart, the fallen self, "the old man,"[5] as the
Scripture calls it, whether it be in the uncon-
verted or in the keenest Christian. It is hard
to believe that these things can proceed from
the heart of ministers, evangelists, and Christian workers, but it is true. The simple truth
is that the only beautiful thing about the
Christian is Jesus Christ. God wants us to recognize that fact as true in our experience, so

[2] Mark 7:21–22. [3] Gal. 5:19–21. [4] Jer. 17:9. [5] Eph. 4:22.

that in true brokenness and self-despair we shall allow Jesus Christ to be our righteousness and holiness and all in all—and that is victory.

Making God a Liar!

Now in face of God's description of the human heart, we can see what it was that the Pharisee did. In saying "I thank Thee that I am not as other men are, extortioners, unjust, adulterers," he was protesting his innocence of the very things that God says are in every heart. He said in effect, "These things are doubtless true of other men—this Publican is even now confessing them—but Lord, not of me!" And in so saying, he was making God a liar, for "if we say we have not sinned, we make him a liar,"[6] because He says we have! Yet I feel sure that he was perfectly sincere in what he said. He really *did* believe that he was innocent of these things. Indeed, he is ascribing his imagined innocence to God, saying, "I thank thee. . . ." God's Word, however, still stood against him. But he just had not seen it. "The penny had not dropped!" If the Publican is beating upon his breast and confessing his sins, it is not because he has sinned worse than the Pharisee. It is simply that the

---

[6] 1 John 1:10.

Publican has seen that what God says is woefully true of him, and the Pharisee has not. The Pharisee still thinks that outward abstinence from certain sins is all that God requires. He has not yet understood that God looks, not on the outward appearance, but on the heart,[7] and accounts the look of lust the equivalent of adultery,[8] the attitude of resentment and hate the same as murder,[9] envy as actual theft, and the petty tyrannies in the home as wicked as the most extortionate dealings in the market.

How often have not we, too, protested our innocence on the many occasions when God has been convicting others, and when He has wanted to convict us too. We have said in effect, "These things may be true of others, but not of me!" and we may have said so quite sincerely. Perhaps we have heard of others who have humbled themselves and have rather despised them for the confessions they have had to make and the things they had to put right in their lives. Or perhaps we have been genuinely glad that they have been blessed. But, whichever it is, we don't feel that we have anything to be broken about ourselves. Beloved, if we feel we are innocent and have nothing to be broken about, it is not that these things are not there but that we have

---

[7] 1 Sam. 16:7.   [8] Matt. 5:27–28.   [9] 1 John 3:15.

not seen them. We have been living in a realm of illusion about ourselves. God must be true in all that He says about us. In one form or another, He sees these things expressing themselves in us (unless we have recognized them and allowed God to deal with them)— unconscious selfishness, pride, and self-congratulation; jealousy, resentment, and impatience; reserve, fears, and shyness; dishonesty and deception; impurity and lust; if not one thing, then another. But we are blind to it. We are perhaps so occupied with the wrong the other man has done us that we do not see that we are sinning against Christ in not being willing to take it with His meekness and lowliness. Seeing so clearly how the other man wants his own way and rights, we are blind to the fact that we want ours just as much; and yet we know there is something missing in our lives. Somehow we are not in vital fellowship with God. We are not spiritually crisp. Our service does not "crackle with the supernatural." Unconscious sin is, nonetheless, sin with God and separates us from Him. The sin in question may be quite a small thing, which God will so readily show us if we are only willing to ask Him.

There is yet another error we fall into when we are not willing to recognize the truth of what God says of the human heart. Not only do we protest our own innocence, but we often protest the innocence of our loved ones. We hate to see them being convicted and humbled and we hasten to defend them. We do not want them to confess anything. We are living in a realm of illusion not only about ourselves, but about them too, and we fear to have it shattered. But we are only defending them against God—making God a liar on their behalf, as we do on our own, and keeping them from entering into blessing, as we do also ourselves.

Only a deep hunger for real fellowship with God will make us willing to cry to God for His all-revealing Light and to obey it when it is given.

Justifying God

That brings us to the Publican. With all that God says about the human heart in our minds, we can see that his confession of sin was simply a justifying of God, an admission that what God said of him was true. Perhaps like the Pharisee, he used not to believe that what God said about man was really true of him. But the Holy Spirit has shown him things in his life which prove God right, and he is broken. Not only does he justify God in all that He has said, but he doubtless justifies God in all the chastening judgments God has brought upon him. Nehemiah's prayer might well have been his: "Howbeit thou art just in all that is brought upon us; for thou hast done right, but we have done wickedly."[10]

This is ever the nature of true confession of sin, true brokenness. It is the confession that my sin is not just a mistake, a slip, a something which is really foreign to my heart ("Not really like me to have such thoughts or do such things!"), but that it is something which reveals the real "I"; that shows me to be the proud, rotten, unclean thing God says I am; that it really *is* like me to have such thoughts and do such things. It was in these terms that David confessed his sin, when he prayed, "Against thee, thee only, have I sinned, and done this evil in thy sight: *that thou mightest be justified when thou speakest, and be clear when thou judgest.*"[11] Let us not fear, then, to make such a confession where God convicts us that we must, thinking that it will "let Jesus down." Rather, the reverse is true, for out of such confession God gets glory, for we declare Him to be right. This brings us to a new experience of victory in Christ, for it declares afresh that "in me (that is, in my

---

[10] Neh. 9:33. [11] Psalm 51:4.

flesh) dwelleth no good thing,"[12] and brings us to a place where we give up trying to make our incorrigible selves holy and where we take Jesus to be our holiness and His life to be our life.

Peace and Cleansing

But the Publican did something more than justify God. He pointed to the sacrifice on the altar, and found peace with God and cleansing from sin as he did so. That comes out in the literal meaning of the words which he uttered, "God be merciful to me, a sinner." In the Greek the words mean literally, "God be propitiated to me, the sinner." The only way by which a Jew knew that God could be propitiated was by a sacrifice, and, in all probability, at that very hour the lamb for the daily burnt offering was being offered up on the altar in the temple.

With us it is the same. A man never comes to this position of brokenness but that God shows him the Divine Lamb on Calvary's cross, putting away his sin by the shedding of His blood. The God who declares beforehand what we are, provides beforehand for our sin. Jesus was the Lamb slain for our sins from the foundation of the world. In Him,

---

[12] Rom. 7:18.

who bore them in meekness, my sins are finished. And as I, in true brokenness, confess
them, and put my faith in His blood, they are
cleansed and gone. Peace with God then
comes into my heart, fellowship with God is
immediately restored, and I walk with Him
in white.

This simple way of being willing to justify
God and see the power of the blood to cleanse
brings within our reach, as never before, a
close walk with Jesus, a constant dwelling
with Him in the Holy of Holies. As we walk
with Him in the Light, He will be showing us
all the time the beginnings of things which, if
allowed to pass, will grieve Him and check
the flow of His life in us—things which are
the expression of that old proud self for which
God has nothing but judgment. We must at
no point protest our innocence of what He
shows us. All along we must be willing to
justify Him and say, "Thou art right, Lord;
that just shows what I am," and be willing to
give it to Him for cleansing. As we do so, we
shall find that His precious blood is continuously cleansing us from sin, and that "the tide
is being continuously healed at its beginning," and Jesus is continuously filling us
with His Spirit. This demands that we must
be men of "a humble and contrite spirit," that

is, men who are willing to be shown the smallest thing. But such are the ones, God says, who "dwell with Him in the high and holy place,"[13] and who experience continuous revival.

There then is our choice—to protest our innocence and go down to our house unblessed, dry of soul, and out of touch with God. Or to justify God and to enter into peace, fellowship, and victory through the blood of Jesus.

---

[13] Isa. 57:15.

· 11 ·

Forty Years Later
A Personal Interview
with the Author

*This is a transcript of three interviews between David Mains and Roy Hession on the subject of revival and his book **The Calvary Road**, recorded in August 1988 and broadcast in November of the same year, which was the Jubilee year of The Chapel of the Air, Wheaton, Illinois.*

DAVID MAINS: Hi, good friend. I'm David Mains, greeting you again this anniversary month in the Chapel of the Air. A new beginning—that does sound good, doesn't it? "Being infused with fresh life," that's what that word *revival* means: "life coming back again." One of the most popular and helpful books on this subject came out way back in 1950. Only a little over a hundred pages, it was called *The Calvary Road* and it's still popular today. It was written by Roy Hession, evangelist. And Roy Hession of the West Country, near Plymouth in England, is my Chapel guest this visit and will be for the next two days.

Roy, what has been your experience with personal revival? Can you share that with us?

ROY HESSION: I would be very happy to because it is the one theme that's been preoccupying me for the last few years. I do evangelistic work, but above all I am concerned for the revival of the church, inasmuch as I had to have, and still have to have, an experience of revival . . . and that continuously. I had been doing evangelistic work full time—and there is a story as to how I was called to that, but I don't want to touch on that. I had had some very fruitful years and many had turned to the Lord . . . much of it, of course, in Great Britain. Then, after a certain high peak, I found a decline set in and I somehow lost the power of the Holy Spirit and the liberty and power which I had once known in proclaiming the gospel. And what I did was to try to make up for the lack of that power by my own efforts. I prayed longer; I studied harder; I preached more vehemently, but all to no avail: that lack persisted. I little knew at the time, but that very state of decline was making me a fit candidate for the grace of God. It was Finney who said, "Revival always presupposes a declension. Therefore if a man can't own up to declension, he is no candidate for revival personally." Well, I was experiencing the declension, but as yet was not willing to admit it. Then it was that God sent back to England some missionaries and African leaders from Uganda, Ruanda and Kenya, and they came back expressly to share with the Christians of England what they had been learning in revival. This was 1947.

DAVID: And that was from the East African revival which had been going on?

ROY: Yes, they came back from the revival in East Africa, not merely to have a furlough, but to share with us what they had been learning in it. It had been going on for years and it still goes on today, which is over fifty years. But the beginnings had begun and already a discernible movement was taking place. These missionaries themselves were not the fathers of the revival as much as some of its many children. And very often they were brought into the fullness of the blessing of the gospel of Christ through the testimony and challenge of the Africans, can you believe it? That revival to this day is far more led by the Africans than by the missionaries.

DAVID: Now how did this touch you?

ROY: Well, that revival touched me because

I invited these men to my conference, to be the speakers, and I little knew that they'd get more concerned for the leader of that conference than for anybody else. And they really began to counsel me. They began to share the little they had begun to see of my need—and I was in a state of need! I had come into a state of declension. And I remember one of them said, "Roy, you need to repent." I said, "Where do I need to repent?" In all honesty I didn't know—I was working so hard, I was praying so much, I was preaching so strong, doing so much. They said, "Well, we don't know where you need to repent. We could, of course, make a suggestion. You see, we've only just got to know you. But we've got to know enough to be able to suggest at least one place where you might begin, and that's in your relationship with your wife. When we came on the campus, you said, 'Fellows, get in the car, I've got to go to one of the other houses to make some arrangements.' And in that house we saw you talking to a young lady; we didn't know by the way in which you spoke to her whether she was your secretary or your wife. We suggest you might begin there, because revival for us began in our most intimate relationship . . . in the home." Well, I took it to heart. I had a special "victorious life" message, which had ceased to work. And I said to myself, I'm going to park that message and am just going to respond to current light as it comes. That current light came to show me sin where I hadn't seen it before, and I began on a path of repentance. Yes, with my wife—my attitude toward her. You see, I was a tense man—and a tense man is a difficult person to live with. And I had to see it wasn't her fault in this or that, it was mine; and I began to take that to Jesus. And I the evangelist, quite well known in England, began on a new path of calling sin *sin*, and a path of repentance—and that, of course, in turn meant I had to find a new power in the blood of Jesus Christ to deal with all the things that the light was showing in my life.

DAVID: And you deal with that so beautifully in this book, *The Calvary Road*. Again, it's been out many years and still continues to be a help to people. Thank you for sharing so personally. There is a certain sense in which that transparency is a part of revival. God works with you and then you share that and He is able to work with others. I appreciate that. We've started out on a good footing here and that makes me very comfortable.

In the very beginning of your book you continue this theme. You use the word *broken-ness*. You say that brokenness is always one of those first parts of revival. I need you to define what you mean by "brokenness" when you use the term.

ROY: I think it is very important to do that because it does occur, of course, in Scripture—several places—where the broken and the contrite heart is spoken of. But unless we really explain what we mean, that word could become a cliché. People could get the impression of "many tears" and "terrible experience." It's nothing of the sort; it is a matter of the will. Brokenness is the opposite to hardness. Hardness says "It's your fault," brokenness says "It's mine." And it's a struggle for a man to be willing to say that, especially when he has professed so loudly that he's right . . . the other fellows have got him wrong. When God wins a victory in his life he says, "Fellows, *I'm* the one who is wrong." They too may be wrong, but that's not his business. He is the one who's wrong and very often the wrong is his reaction to their wrong. They may be wrong in their actions, but he is wrong in his reactions—his anger, his resentment, his jealousy—and nothing is gained by confessing the other fellows' sins. It's got to be *me,* and brokenness is *me* being willing to do that.

people, with the option of doing things right this time. Sound good? Join us in our Jubilee celebration here in the Chapel of the Air. Hi again, good friend. David Mains here with my guest, Roy Hession. We have reprinted chapter 2 of your book, Roy, in our monthly *Reveille* magazine. That chapter is called "Cups Running Over" and it is a word picture about new life in Christ. Now I want you to explain for us, please, what you mean by "cups running over." Okay?

ROY: This is an expression that became current in the early days of revival in East Africa. That revival, by the way, continues unabated on a larger scale than ever before, although they have had many painful vicissitudes. "Cups running over" did become a phrase. It is, of course, taken from Psalm 23: "My cup runneth over." And it was used, and might still be used, to express the joy and the liberty that's come to a person who has been newly washed and made clean in the blood of Jesus Christ. It was first used by a dear friend of mine, Dr. Joe Church, who now lives in retirement in England. He was one of the early leaders of the revival and he gave a special picture at a great open-air conference (we call them conventions) in a natural amphitheatre. Thousands and thousands were there, and he gave the picture of Jesus coming into that gathering with a golden water pot on His shoulder in which was the Water of Life. And he suggested that if they needed to be filled with the Holy Spirit that they hold out their hand in the shape of a cup, and he bade them imagine that Jesus was coming down the rows with the golden water pot and He would tilt the water pot and fill the cup until it ran over with the Water of Life. However, he said, He might come to some cup, look in and shake His head sadly and pass on, because that cup was stained and dirty. And before He could fill that cup He would have to cleanse those stains of sin. Some people might say, "Well, this is not sin, it's just part of my make-up." "No," He says, "you must call it sin." And as you confess it, He cleanses it with His blood and He fills what He has cleansed with the Water of Life. And that came to be a phrase; when a man was newly cleansed he would say, "Praise the Lord, my cup's now running over"—but only because the blood of Jesus had been applied.

DAVID: You do so well with that in your book *The Calvary Road*, in chapter 2, "Cups Running Over." In fact, we reprinted chapter 2 in our monthly *Reveille* magazine, and here is this picture in detail of Christ filling one's life . . . but not being able to do that if sin is there. Are you talking about big sins like murdering someone, or possibly committing adultery, say, or thieving, or are you talking about everyday sins that would keep Christ from filling that cup?

ROY: Everyday sins, the big and the little. There is no difference in His sight. And many of them are not sins of action but sins of reaction. Maybe the wrong action was somebody else's, but my reaction to their action is wrong too. Jealousy, or anger, or resentment—that is enough to stain the cup and prevent Him from filling it. But if I confess those things as sin, the blood of Jesus Christ cleanses from all sin.

DAVID: Do you think the average Christian today regularly does confess sin, or is this something that is somewhat foreign to Christian thinking?

ROY: Well, it was a bit foreign to my own, evangelist that I was. I wouldn't have said at that time that repentance was an essential part of my Christian life. And for that reason the blood of Jesus Christ wasn't all that important to me. But now, this is all my hope and peace, nothing but the blood of Jesus; this is all my righteousness, nothing but the blood of Jesus. And I have been helped to walk this way, calling things by their name and proving there is power, wonder-working power in the blood of Jesus Christ.

DAVID: It's wonderful. In this chapter "Cups Running Over" you use the term regularly. You talk about continuous revival. Now some people think of revival as happening at a point in time and then you can bask in the warmth of what took place. That's not what you're talking about, is it?

ROY: No, continuous. I mean, a thing that is in the past is in the past, it is not affecting me in the present. But Jesus is alive in the present and His blood has never lost its power. This revival movement is the biggest demonstration of continuous revival. They have recently celebrated their fiftieth anniversary of revival. They didn't call it that, but it so happened that certain gatherings were just about the fiftieth year after, and that revival is going on as never before; for one reason, because the blood has never lost its power and they on their part have been willing to go on repenting. Indeed, I have friends who have written to me in the past who have ended their letters, "Yours, repenting and rejoicing."

DAVID: It's wonderful. But let's go back to you personally, Roy. I assume you have held your cup up to Christ just recently, if I may use that word picture. When did you do this and how? . . . just to be very practical for people.

ROY: Well, the Lord recently showed me something that I hadn't really seen as sin. Now that is God's dealings; He shows you something to be sin that you hadn't been seeing as sin. I've been living now for the last few years in a seaside town near Plymouth and it has one of the largest Baptist churches in Great Britain, and that is the church I attend. The minister is a friend of mine, and we've been there the last few years as I have not been filling my calendar up so much as before . . . so I've had many spare Sundays. I have attended that church and, do you know, I haven't appreciated it. I haven't been really *blessed* by it. I haven't enjoyed their style of singing. Oh, it's orthodox, yet I could express reasons—lacks here and lacks there. But the other day the Lord showed me, at the bottom of it all was that I had not been drawn in.

"You," He said, "have been usually out there at the front, but now you're just sitting in the pew." Then some time later I was pre-

paring a message on one of Jesus' parables—
the one that says when you are invited to a
feast, don't sit down in the highest room, but
rather sit in the lowest room. And the Lord
said to me, "You should have loved that lowest place, for there you would have found Me.
I took the lowest place for you. But you have
been restive because you've not been willing
to embrace it happily." I called that sin and
put it under the blood, and I find there's a
new something in my heart because of that
fact. And that has put me on the track of some
other sins in my life, unsuspected forms of
self—and every one of them is sin—but the
blood of Jesus has never lost its power and is
mighty enough, sufficient enough to bring
even me into the fullness of the blessing of
the gospel of Christ again.

DAVID: You live what you preach, don't
you? Bless you, it's so good to have you as a
guest. Have you ever experienced revival
beyond just the personal, Roy? Have you ever
been in a situation where many, many, many
people are experiencing revival, many cups
running over?

ROY: Yes, but I hesitate to try and chalk up
successes; that is one of the tendencies that
I've got to recognize as sin. And if I think too

much about that, that'll be the end of the out-flow. And I think one of the reasons people don't see success more often is that they are wanting it too much. It should be enough to have Jesus, and in Jesus all else. And He will take care of the overflow to others.

DAVID: Beautiful. Your answers are always good. Then, Roy, I have one more question for you. You make this topic sound very simple, the topic of personal revival. Would you say that it really isn't all that complicated?

ROY: It certainly is not complicated and we don't really need to introduce anything else than what we find in Scripture. 1 John 1:7 says, "If we walk in the light, as He is in the light, we have fellowship one with another, and the blood of Jesus Christ, God's Son, cleanses us from all sin." Now in John's writings light and darkness are not vague synonyms for good and evil. Light, rather, is simply that which reveals, darkness that which hides. And God is light, the All-revealing One—and if we are prepared to walk in His light and say yes to what His light may reveal as sin, we'll go on in the light. And if we're prepared to simply walk in the light and say, "Yes, Lord, You're right and I'm wrong on that matter," the blood of Jesus

Christ cleanses us from all sin . . . and we can't be more right with God than what the blood of Jesus makes us when we call sin *sin*. Go on doing it and you'll go on rejoicing.

DAVID: Thank you, Roy Hession. Join me again tomorrow, friend, and we'll explore further this privilege we have of walking with Christ in our everyday world.

Third Interview

DAVID: Roy, you say that if God is to bless the reader through these pages of your book he must come to them with a deep hunger of heart. He must be possessed with a dissatisfaction of the state of the church in general and of himself in particular—especially of himself. Now I've read that in a lot of other places. Why is it that revival so often begins with this sense of dissatisfaction?

ROY: Well, to ask the question is almost to answer it. In the very nature of the case, if you are going to enjoy the meal your wife has prepared for you you've got to have a nice appetite, you've got to be hungry. And perhaps you need to have a few unfortunate experiences of other people's cooking, and then you come back to the one whose cooking you know does satisfy. And the same is true here:

grace is flowing like a river, millions of others have been supplied . . . but *you've* got to be hungry, *you've* got to be in need—and I want to tell you those are the times when I get blessed. I do not get blessed when I read my Bible as a matter of duty for a daily quiet time. Rather, when I come feeling bad, *those* are the times when it speaks, livingly! And again and again I have to say to the Lord, "I want to tell You something: I'm not in spiritual good shape." "Just fine," says the Lord, "anything more?" "Well, I haven't got much peace." "Anything more? Come on, let it all out." And when I come like that, grace meets me; because when I admit that I'm in that position, in the very nature of the case I become a candidate for that marvelous grace of our loving Lord, grace that exceeds our sin and our guilt. Grace is not God's reward for the faithful, it's His gift for the empty and the feeble and the failing. When I am feeling like that, I'm just the one who is going to be blessed.

DAVID: Take that phrase, "grace meets me." Explain what you mean by that for someone who maybe doesn't know what grace is.

ROY: Grace is the undeserved favor of God, and you are no candidate for grace unless you are undeserving. You can't be too down, too wrong, for grace. That's where Jesus gets His glory; not in the number of good Christians He pats on the back, but in the failures He restores.

DAVID: Beautiful! Now in *The Calvary Road* you talk about the self-satisfied Pharisee and the dissatisfied Publican in the parable Christ told. Do you remember that chapter, "Protesting Our Innocence"?

ROY: Yes, well, that is what we all naturally do. We naturally justify ourselves; therefore you're no candidate for *God* to justify. God justifies—listen—the *un*godly. Have you ever heard a greater apparent contradiction? God who justifies the *un*godly! He who commands earthly judges "You shall justify the innocent but condemn the wicked"[1] is here doing the very opposite. "I'm setting My court of grace—it's in order to justify those who are *un*godly." He declares those to be right who admit they are wrong. And to see that, gives you a bigger incentive than ever before to take the place of the wrong one.

DAVID: So all of self becomes a hindrance to revival, doesn't it? Whether it's selfishness, or self-effort, self-indulgence, self-pity, or self-righteousness.

---

[1] Deuteronomy 25:1.

ROY: Yes, the things you've mentioned all begin with self. They are all sinful and it's not without significance that the central letter of the little word sin is "I."

DAVID: It's a big problem, isn't it, to somehow get beyond that. Dissatisfaction—that's a good thing; when we are dissatisfied we aspire for something more, and God fills that in us. If we don't have any dissatisfaction we don't aspire for anything more.

ROY: Well, I don't like the word "aspire"; that looks as if I'm going to get better. I come empty; my dissatisfaction draws me to the One who has got something good for those who confess they are failures.

DAVID: I agree with what you say; it's a good correction. Your book *The Calvary Road* is about revival. You use that word a lot, but you don't equate the ongoing experience of revival with an emotional high. Now, is revival ever emotional?

ROY: Of course, life is full of emotion; sometimes sad, sometimes glad, sometimes shouting. And you're given good grounds for which to shout and praise; not that I'm wanting people to shout, necessarily, but there is solid ground for it. When grace shows me that my righteousness is absolutely unassailable before God in the Person of Jesus Christ, that I've boldness to enter the Holiest by the blood of Jesus, that I needn't go struggling and striving and mourning—that's something worth praising for! It isn't just an unaccountable emotion, that's the point. You're given solid, rational grounds for your joy.

DAVID: That's really well said; your answers are wonderful. Let's talk just a little while about the blood of Jesus. You come back to that again and again. I am not sure the average person is conscious of the value of Christ's blood in terms of daily living. Do you sense Christ's blood being operative in your life on, say, a daily basis?

ROY: Yes, I don't think you could have asked me a more important question. What is meant by the blood of Jesus? Some people are a bit squeamish when they hear preaching about the blood. And when they are called upon to sing about the blood they lose their enthusiasm—because some people can't bear the sight of blood. The first time a nurse is present at an operation she will probably faint; and yet the Christian is all the time glorying in the cross and in the blood of Jesus Christ. Now what does it mean? There is a famous Old Testament incident, the Passover. The first-born died in every house except where that particular Jewish home had taken a lamb, slain it, and sprinkled its blood upon the door—not only slain the lamb, but sprinkled the blood, for God had said, "When I see the blood I will pass over you." Note that in the instructions given for the slaying of the lamb and the sprinkling of its blood these words occur: "And the blood shall be to you for a token." A token of what? Apparently it wasn't the physical blood that was important, it was that of which that blood was a token. What is that? It was a token of judgment met. God said, "Judgment is coming on every house"; but the blood said, "A lamb's been slain here; the judgment that should have fallen on the eldest son has fallen on the lamb, and it can't come in a second time." So the blood is a token of that fact, that judgment has been met. It's as simple as that; it always speaks of the finished work of Christ.

There's a lovely hymn we sing in England:

> *Jesus the sinner's Friend,*
> *We hide ourselves in Thee,*
> *God looks upon Thy sprinkled blood,*
> *It is our only plea.*

Yes, the blood is a token that all the judgment that was *my* due has already been met and finished with.

DAVID: Amen, and that's true in our lives on a daily basis, isn't it?

ROY: Yes, indeed! There's the shedding of the blood once for all, but we've got to sprinkle it by faith, and claim it for everything that would otherwise put us out of fellowship with God.

DAVID: Am I out of line in asking you what your age is?

ROY: Eighty.

DAVID: You're eighty; my, and this was written in 1950. That's a long time ago. You were optimistic about what God was doing among His people when you wrote *The Calvary Road*. Are you still optimistic about what God is doing?

ROY: Yes, I never knew, or thought, that He would use that book as He has used it. I've been absolutely staggered. It is only because—not because of the book but the working of the Lord and the hunger of the saints of God. They are hungry as never before, and I want to spend my remaining days in helping to lead people back to Calvary, back to the blood, back to liberty, back to revival.

DAVID: Amen. And the continuing popularity of the book is a good sign that people are still listening to your message, the message about Christ and His blood. I have one last question for you, Roy Hession—how good to have you here. Its been a privilege to talk to you these last three days. These three visits have gone by much too quickly. In closing, do you have any thoughts that can kind of summarize what we've been saying about revival?

ROY: Well, first it must begin with the individual; not with the other fellow, but with me. He may be wrong, but I'm wrong too, probably in my reactions to him. Therefore as far I am concerned, it begins with me. Then secondly, I think I need to repeat what Finney said: "Revival always presupposes a declension"; and therefore, in the nature of the case, the man who is the most ready to admit there has been a declension is the more likely to be a candidate for revival. It's got to begin with the admission of my need. I would like to say very forcibly, revival is not a green valley getting greener, but a valley full of dry bones (Ezekiel 37) being made to live again, and those bones to stand up a mighty army. Not a good Christian becoming a better Christian, but a man who is prepared to confess "Mine is a valley full of dry bones" being made to live again. I've heard people admit it—and it's broken their hearts. "Mine is a valley full of dry bones; I'm a minister, maybe, but it's a valley full of dry bones!" Splendid, brother; praise the Lord, that you were ready to confess it. If you but realize it, that gives you your qualification for Jesus. He belongs to you if only by your failures; He's a specialist in sin, is Jesus. This is where He excels. When you take that place, you're a candidate *and you are not going to be disappointed.*

DAVID: Sounds very much like your book again. What a great adventure, walking with Christ in our everyday world.

By the Same Author

THE WAY OF THE CROSS   Paperback

This version of *The Calvary Road* has been prepared especially for those whose first language is not English, and is sent out with the hope that it will prove especially useful for deaf readers who are anxious to explore the deeper meanings of the message of the cross.

WE WOULD SEE JESUS   Paperback

This book seeks to be only about the Lord Jesus Christ Himself. Seeing Him is enough. Seeing Him we are convicted of sin, broken, cleansed, filled with the Spirit, set free from bondage and revived. Each aspect of Christian experience is made real in us just by seeing Him.

FORGOTTEN FACTORS   Paperback

The author points out the forgotten factors in sexual sins, those matters which are so often missed when people try to get right—the wrong done to another, the multiplied duplicities, the wrong done to one's own body, the wrong done to God—and shows these factors in all the main forms of sexual misbehavior.

"WHEN I SAW HIM . . ." —where revival begins
Paperback

"In the following pages I invite the reader to look with me at four men of old (in one of the cases in question, a group of men) who saw the Lord, and at the effects the visions had on them. I do so because the particular revelations of the Lord they had are the same revelations of Him we need, and when we have them they will have the same effect on us as they had on them."

GOOD NEWS FOR BAD PEOPLE   Paperback

"*Good News for Bad People* for me exactly defines what the grace of our God is to sinners, and no words could better convey the message of this book. But it is really a handbook of revival theology, for although its title might make it appear to be solely an evangelistic book, the 'bad people' of the title can often be converted persons."

BE FILLED NOW   Stapled Booklet

A concise, practical study of the person and work of the Holy Spirit. In eight short chapters the author highlights key truths which should challenge every believing Christian.